THE TOP ⑩ RULES FOR SUCCESS

Rules to Succeed in Business and Life
from **Titans**, **Billionaires**, and **Leaders**
who Changed the World.

BY: EVAN CARMICHAEL

ISBN: 978-1-7751263-0-0

DO YOU WANT FREE BONUSES?

Thank you for buying my latest book!

I want to show my thanks by giving you some free bonuses.

Woo hoo ☺

If you email either your receipt, a picture of you with the book, or a link to a social media post you created of you with the book to top10@evancarmichael.com, I'll send you a number of free bonuses for as long as the bonus program is running, including:

- **The 3 Bonus Rules.** These rules didn't quite make the Top 10 list but were repeated consistently and are great reminders to live by and apply to your life and business.

- **Motivational cheat sheet poster PDF** of the Top 10 Rules that you can print and put up in your home or office as a daily reminder of the habits you want to keep top of mind.

- **Social media shoutout.** I'll personally thank you for your support at the end of one of my YouTube videos.

- **The next 10 legends.** This book has rules from 40 leaders but my original idea for the book was 50. I'll send you the other 10 in a PDF download. They are: A.P.J. Abdul Kalam, Bruce Lee, George Carlin, Michael Jordan, Dwayne "The Rock" Johnson, Dave Grohl, Floyd Mayweather, Muhammad Ali, Paul McCartney, and Anna Wintour.

Please make sure to email your receipt or a picture of you with the book, or a social media post you created about the book to top10@evancarmichael.com.

Thank you once again for your support!

Much love,

Evan.
#Believe

THE 40

Don't Read this Book Like a Book!

Think of this book like meeting the world's greatest mentors and them giving you a daily, personal challenge with specific advice on how to be the *best version of yourself.*

One of the best ways to be great is to surround yourself with greatness. The more you are around successful people, ideas, and mindsets, the more successful you will become.

My best advice to you in picking up this book is *do not read it like a book.* Don't just read it cover to cover. You'll blow through it too quickly, miss too many lessons, and not take enough action.

I want you to get results from reading this book. I want you to move closer to building the dream business and dream life that you want for yourself. Here's how to get it: *Every day, start your day by reading just one page of this book, then take action.* That's it. One page, then action.

Reading one page every morning does a few things for you:

First, it's easy to do. It's just one page! You have time every day to read one page in a book.

Second, it's motivation. Being around successful people who are sharing their wisdom will rub off on you. If you do it daily then you consistently get genius coming into you. Starting your day with it sets you up for a great day of being bold, taking action, and being productive.

Third, it's effective. The best gift you can give yourself is to take action. Don't just read. Do something! Each page has two lessons. After you read one page, think about how you can apply one or both of those lessons to your life or business today. Even if it's just a tiny, seemingly insignificant action, do something. Every day you take two genius ideas and apply them.

Don't let that knowledge and wisdom go to waste by blowing through the content. *One page. Every day. Then take action.* Your world will explode forward if you do.

Why I Wrote This Book

It started with my YouTube channel. *I wanted to learn from successful entrepreneurs* and would spend hours watching videos of people like Elon Musk only to find that in a day's worth of footage there was 15 to 20 minutes of gold nuggets to take away.

It wasn't Elon's fault. In those videos he was talking about things that weren't relevant to me or being asked questions by reporters that I didn't find interesting. He wasn't setting out to create a 'How to be successful' guide for people *so I had to piece it together.*

I thought to myself, 'Man, someone should put together the highlights of his *best advice and compress it down* to the 15 or 20 minutes of amazing value.' And, like most entrepreneurs, instead of complaining about a problem, I set out to find a solution.

I started myself, and later brought on a team to sift through the hours upon hours of content on different successful people and mix together their best wisdom. I called it the Top 10 Rules for Success series because it was *my take on their best advice.* It was what I personally learned from them by watching the videos.

The idea for the book came because sometimes you don't have an Internet connection. Sometimes you're travelling. Sometimes you're underground on the subway. Sometimes you just want the feel of a book in your hands.

And so I went through my YouTube channel, pulled together the *most popular 40 people* I've profiled, compressed their thoughts down to half a page per rule, and served them up for you to think about and apply to your life and business.

This book starts with a *summary of the most popular rules for success.* It basically takes the 400 rules from the 40 people profiled and condenses it down even further to the 10 most commonly discussed ideas. Then it goes into each of the 40 people, with my take on their Top 10 Rules for Success individually.

I hope this journey helps you as much as it has helped me.

THE TOP (10) RULES FOR SUCCESS

RULE 1:
Follow Your Passion

RULE 2:
Have Self-Awareness

RULE 3:
Raise Your Standards

RULE 4:
Focus

RULE 5:
Work Hard

RULE 6:
Embrace Failure

RULE 7:
Ignore the #LittleMan

RULE 8:
Build a Team

RULE 9:
Model Success

RULE 10:
#Believe

Please see instructions on *page iii* to get the link to a full size PDF poster of this image.

Rule #1: Follow Your Passion

"The key point is: you've got to enjoy what you do every day."

– Bill Gates

Follow your passion. Do what you love. Pursue your purpose. There are lots of ways of pointing at the same thing but after the years I've spent researching the most successful entrepreneurs, actors, artists, singers, writers, innovators, and leaders, the number one, most consistent piece of advice from all of them is that you need to follow your passion.

If you want to find ultimate success and make your mark then you need to ***find the thing that you would do even if you never got paid for it.*** Find the thing that you can be so obsessed about that you'll keep going even if doesn't make practical sense, even if the people around you say you're crazy, even if it has a low probability of succeeding.

You keep going because you need to keep going. Because it's a part of you. Because you'll be an army of one to will this idea of yours into existence. Because you don't want to look back on your life and realize that you quit on one of the most important projects of your life. Having the courage to make the big decision with your heart and say, 'yes', while your head says, 'no', is tough. But that's the courage that you're going to need to create a new, better world and turn your dream into a reality.

You don't get to be the best by doing what you hate or just find okay. ***You become the best by loving what you do more than anyone else and following that passion through.***

Rule #2: Have Self-Awareness

"Way too many people are going to spend the next 30, 40 years of their lives, trying to check the boxes of the things that they're not as good at, and you're going to waste a load of time, and lose."

– Gary Vaynerchuk

Following your passion isn't enough. It's just your ticket in. It doesn't guarantee your success.

The next step successful people take is having self-awareness (like finding and applying your One Word). They understand what they're good at, what they have Michael Jordan level talent at, and they pursue that instead of trying to do everything themselves.

They plan a schedule, work environment, and team around themselves, even if it leads to an unconventional structure. It's not how most people do things, but it works for them, and that's the point.

Having the self-awareness to understand how you work best and then build a business around it gives you the best chance at success.

It also means understanding that you are different and not shying away from that just so you can fit in with others. Your difference is your power. Having that *self-awareness allows you to be authentic* while others are faking their way through life.

It allows you to speak up while others are too afraid to act. It allows you to trust your instincts while others are waiting for the approval of other people. The hardest fight is understanding what the best version of you looks like. With that clarity, the world will conspire to help you get it.

Rule #3: Raise Your Standards

"Develop the habit of giving more than what you're paid for. Develop the habit of setting standards that others will be measured by. Do not go where the path may lead, but go where there's no path and leave a trail."

– Les Brown

There's a reason why it's commonly said that you'll end up *being the average of your five closest friends.* It's because you are a product of your environment.

If you have people with a poor mindset around you, if you're surrounded by others who default to scarcity, limiting beliefs, and complaining, *guess what you are most likely to become?*

It's really hard to stand up to your friends and tell them that instead of blaming their parents, education, or the government that they should take responsibility for their lives and raise their standards for what they will no longer tolerate in their lives.

Good luck with that conversation. It's hard and that's why most people don't do it and *forever stay where they are, blaming* others for their situation.

The self-made successes profiled in this book almost all come from challenging situations and environments.

There are a few exceptions, but for the most part these people all came from more challenging upbringings and situations than you're currently facing right now.

If they can raise their standards and achieve massive success, so can you, once you truly decide that you want to.

Rule #4: Focus

"I'm saying no to a lot of ideas because as a CEO, I have to say no to opportunities, because if I say yes, I probably get 5,000 opportunities everyday."

– Jack Ma

So many entrepreneurs are great dreamers. We love coming up with ideas for products and services that could make the world better. And since we're so good at coming up with ideas we also tend to bounce from one idea to the next. Constantly starting one thing and then stopping it to move on to the next new idea.

Success in any field comes from focus. An obsessive, dedicated, absolute focus to see your mission through. It often means seeing very little results at the beginning despite you putting in an insane amount of time. It often means turning away other ideas or giving them to someone else which might have brought you some short term income. It often means dealing with the judgment of other people who don't understand your mission or why you're on it.

If you want to become world class at anything, it requires focus. *You can have the highest standards in the world but if you're not focused in your approach to reach them, you never will.*

Take a look at your calendar. *Pay attention to how you're spending your time.* What percentage of your daily activities are helping you achieve your main goal? Eliminate the waste. Free up your time to allow you to accomplish something big.

Stop jumping from idea to idea and just focus. That's where the magic will happen.

Rule #5: Work Hard

> "I will not be outworked. Period. You might have more talent than me, you might be smarter than me, you might be sexier than me but if we get on the treadmill together, there is two things; you're getting off first, or I'm going to die. It's really that simple."
>
> – Will Smith

Working hard is another must-have if you want to become a success. Forget about the 4-hour workweek. Forget about trying to make passive income. Yes, you want to work smart. Yes, you want to model success to shortcut your path... **AND you need to work hard.** Look at anybody who has had success that you look up to. They put in the hard work to get there.

Of all the rules, working hard is the one that people find most difficult to accept. You're constantly looking for shortcuts. You're looking for ways to automate things. You're looking for ways to delegate things. That's great. And you should keep doing that. But the goal of freeing up your time is so that you can use the extra time that you now have to focus on your big goal and continue working hard.

Quite often the people at the top aren't the most naturally talented. They just outworked everyone else. **Hard work beats talent when talent doesn't work hard.**

This applies to every area of your life. If you want to be a better spouse, work harder at it. If you want to be a better parent, work harder at it. And if you want to be a more successful entrepreneur, then you definitely need to work harder at it.

Forever and ever. **There is no retirement when you're truly committed.**

Rule #6: Embrace Failure

"You must fail 100 times to succeed once, that's part of it. No one succeeds the first time. I had to teach myself early on, expect to fail, expect it, covet it, welcome it, it's going to happen. But it's not a permanent state."

– Sylvester Stallone

Most people are so afraid to fail that they don't even try, and that's the biggest failure of all.

When you first start anything, you're going to fail. When you first try to snowboard, you will fall. When you first try to learn French, you will mispronounce every single word. And when you first start on your entrepreneurial journey, you're going to make many mistakes. Because you don't know what you're doing... *yet.* It's normal.

The key is just to fail small. Don't take out a massive loan that you'll be repaying for the rest of your life. Take that big idea that you have and find the smallest possible way to get started... and start!

If you're failing, it means you're trying something. And if you keep following your passion, focusing, and working hard, eventually you'll hit on something big that works. But it only comes through action.

You don't have to take a big risk but if you take no risk at all, *if you wait until you have 100% of the information, then it's too late.* Your window will have closed. Someone else will be out there making tons of money off of your idea and it's because they were willing to embrace failure while you weren't. Don't let that happen.

Rule #7: Ignore the #LittleMan

"Think of the amount of time that is wasted on negative energy, wondering what other people think of you. What they think of you really doesn't make any difference. It's what you think of you that makes a difference."

– Bob Proctor

The #LittleMan is a reference to my first book, Your One Word. *The #LittleMan is the person in your life who tells you all the reasons why your ideas won't work* and instead of helping you build up, they try to tear you down. Sometimes it's out of love, sometimes out of jealousy, and sometimes we do it to ourselves.

Part of why we fear failure so much isn't just that the idea we had didn't work as expected. It's that *we're worried about failing in front of other people.*

What will the people around you, your friends, your parents, your family think when you fail? How will they see you? What will they say?

You will never have the success you're after if you're living your life according to other people's expectations.

When you're growing up you do what your parents tell you to do. But at some point you need to decide that this is your life! You're going to live it and do what you want instead of trying to please the people around you.

Do you want to be 30 and still living your life according to what your parents want? How about when you're 40? Or 50? Or 60? At what point do *you decide to embrace who you are and live your version of your life and ignore the #LittleMan?*

Rule #8: Build a Team

"This idea that it's a person. It's never a person. It's always a team and the most important thing, if you are an entrepreneur trying to build something is you need to build a really good team and that's what I spend a lot of my time on."
– Mark Zuckerberg

You can't do anything major on your own. Behind every successful person is a team, whether you see them or not. Once you have the self awareness to understand what it is that you have Michael Jordan level talent at, then building a team allows you to hand over the tasks that you're not best suited for to people who love doing them.

Building a great team starts with a mindset. You first accept that you can't do everything yourself. Accept that you don't need to be the best at everything. Accept that you want people on your team who are ***better than you at most of the things*** needed to run the business.

Like everything else, start small, but start. Your first hire can be on a part time basis. You aren't spending a lot of money and you get to practice your management skills.

Remember, you're managing a human being with passions, desires, hopes, and dreams. ***Your job as a leader is to help them uncover their potential*** and stretch them to grow, not just give them tasks because it saves you time.

As you grow, the amount that you contribute to the business shrinks compared to what your team creates so bringing on skilled and passionate people, as well as ***managing your office culture will be critical to your success.***

Rule #9: Model Success

"You've got to go back, because over the past 15 years there's so many different businesses that have tried and failed. You have to go back and find those and learn from those. You've got to understand all the implications and you have to learn from history."

– Mark Cuban

Whatever you're trying to accomplish, whatever your big goal is, whatever huge obstacle is in front of you, someone has figured it out before. If you try to figure it all out on your own, you're going to lose. If you study the success clues that others have left before you, **they can shortcut your path** to achieving your mission.

Modeling success can come from mentors who you meet face to face. **Reach out to successful business owners in your area**, ask them for 15 minutes of their time. Get their advice and then go implement it before going back for more advice.

Mentors love giving back to the next generation but they hate wasting their time, which is what most mentees do. You'll stand out by actually doing the work.

You can also learn from aspirational mentors who you have never met and may never meet. You can read their biographies, listen to their interviews, or watch their Top 10 Rules for Success videos. **Study people in your industry who have made it as well as your heroes outside the industry.**

If you're in the shoe business but love Oprah Winfrey you can learn from her success and apply it to your shoe business. Finally, get online. Chances are one of your heroes is on social media hosting a live chat. Ask your question and start modeling success.

Rule #10: #Believe

> "My grandmother was a maid, that's all she ever knew. The only real expectation she held for me was that I would one day become a maid. I just, no matter what, believed that there was something bigger, greater, more for me."
>
> – Oprah Winfrey

This rule is my personal favorite. *#Believe is my One Word* and it's true that whether you believe you can or can't do something, you're right.

There are so many talented, amazing, creative people out there who have passion, commitment, and genius inside them.

They just don't believe that they can make their dreams happen, and so they don't. Meanwhile *others with less talent rise to the top because they believed that they could.*

We've all had moments of boldness and I encourage you to *think about what triggered that boldness.* Maybe you were watching a video. Maybe you were reading a book. Maybe you were meditating.

It doesn't matter what it was that triggered your bold self-confidence, just figure out what it is. And then *start your day with it every day.* Instead of randomly having it happen to you, plan for it. Consistently.

If you start your day with courageous self-belief every day for the next year, *you will not recognize* the business and the life that you will create for yourself one year from today. So get building and start believing!

THE TOP 400 RULES

"You know what they say about people who don't learn from history..." – Mark Cuban

"Apple, its core value is that we believe that people with passion can change the world for the better." – Steve Jobs

- Entrepreneur, inventor, and industrial designer
- Was co-founder, Chairman, and CEO of Apple
- Recognized as a pioneer of the microcomputer revolution
- Had a net worth of over $8 billion in 2010
- Considered a master of innovation and a design perfectionist

Rule #1: Don't Live a Limited Life

"When you grow up, you tend to get told that the world is the way it is. And your life is just to live your life inside the world, try not to bash into the walls too much, try to have a nice family life, have fun, save a little money. But that's a very limited life. Life can be much broader once you discover one simple fact, and that is that *everything around you that you call life was made up by people that were no smarter than you.* And you can change it, you can influence it, you can build your own things that other people can use.

And the minute that you understand that *you can poke life and that you can change it,* you can mold it. That's maybe the most important thing, is to shake off this erroneous notion that life is there and you're just going to live in it, versus embrace it, change it, improve it, make your mark upon it. I think that's very important, and however you learn that, once you learn it, you'll want to change life and make it better, because it's kind of messed up in a lot of ways. Once you learn that, you will never be the same again."

Rule #2: Have Passion

"People say you have to have a lot of passion for what you're doing, and it's totally true. And the reason is because it's so hard, that if you don't, any rational person would give up. It's really hard. And you have to do it over a sustained period of time. *So if you don't love it, if you're not having fun doing it, and you don't really love it, you're going to give up.* And that's what happens to most people actually. If you really look at the ones that ended up being successful in the eyes of society, and the ones that didn't, oftentimes it's the ones that are successful love what they did so they could persevere when it got really tough.

And the ones that didn't love it quit, because they are sane. Who would want to put up with this stuff if they didn't love it? So it's a lot of hard work, and it's *a lot of worrying constantly*, and if you don't love it, you're going to fail. So you've got to love it, you've got to have passion."

3

Rule #3: Focus

"We try to hire really smart people, but we have a very simple organization, and we try to focus and do very few things well.

And focusing is hard because **focusing doesn't mean saying, 'yes.' It means saying, 'no.'**

We decide not to do a lot of things so we can focus on a handful of things and do them well."

Rule # 4. Don't Sell Crap

[Excerpt from an interview with Mark Parker, shortly after he became CEO of Nike]

"Interviewer: When you first got the job as CEO you got a call from Steve Jobs, and he offered you some advice?

Mark Parker: Long story short, he said, 'Hey, congratulations, that's great. You're going to do a great job.' And I said 'Well, do you have any advice?' And he said 'No, no, you're doing great.'

And there is a pause and he goes, 'Well I do have some advice. Nike makes some of the best product in the world.

I mean products that you lust after. Absolutely beautiful stunning products.

But you also make a lot of crap.'

He said, **'Just get rid of the crappy stuff and focus on the good stuff.'**

And then I expected a little pause and a laugh, but there was a pause but no laugh.

And he was absolutely right."

Rule #5: Build a Great Team

"The greatest people are self-managing, they don't need to be managed. Once they know what to do, they will go and figure out how to do it, and they don't need to be managed at all. *What they need is a common vision*, and that's what leadership is.

We wanted people that were insanely great at what they did, who had at the tips of their fingers, and in their passion, the latest understanding of where technology was, and what we can do with that technology, and who wanted to bring that to lots of people.

So the neatest thing that happens is, when you get a core group of ten great people, it becomes self-policing as to who they let into that group, so I consider the *most important job of someone like myself is recruiting.*

We agonized over hiring. We had interviews, they would start at nine or ten in the morning and go through dinner. New interviewees would talk to everybody in the building at least once, and maybe a couple times, and then come back for another round of interviews. And then we'd all get together and talk about it."

Rule #6: Don't Do it for the Money

"I was worth over a million dollars when I was 23, and over 10 million dollars when I was 24 and over 100 million dollars when I was 25. And it wasn't that important, because I never did it for the money.

I think money is a wonderful thing because it enables you to do things, enables you to invest in ideas that don't have a short term payback and things like that. But, especially at that point in my life, it was not the most important thing.

The most important thing was the company, the people, the products we were making, what we were going to enable people to do with these products. So I didn't think about it a great deal. You know I never sold any stock, I really believed that the company would do really well over the long term."

Rule #7: Be Proud of Your Products

"Our goal is to make the best personal computers in the world and make products we are proud to sell and would recommend to our family and friends.

And we want to do that at the lowest prices we can, but I have to tell you, there's some stuff in our industry that we wouldn't be proud to ship.

That we wouldn't **be proud to recommend to our family and friends,** and we can't do it. We just can't ship junk. So there are thresholds we can't cross because of who we are. But we want to make the best personal computers in our industry.

The difference is, we don't offer stripped down, lousy products. We just don't offer categories of products like that. If you move those aside and **compare us with our competitors, I think we compare pretty favorably.**"

Rule #8: Build Around Customers

"One of the things I've always found is that you've got to **start with the customer experience and work backwards** to the technology. You can't start with the technology and try to figure out where you're going to try to sell it. I've made this mistake probably more than anybody else in this room.

And I've got the scar tissue to prove it. And I know it is the case. And as we've tried to come up with a strategy and a vision for Apple it started with what **incredible benefits can we give to the customer,** where can we take the customer.

Not starting with, let's sit down with the engineers and figure out what awesome technology we have, and then how are we going to market that.

And I think that's the right path to take."

Rule #9: Marketing is About Values *[Evan's Fav]*

"To me, *marketing is about values*. This is a very complicated world, it's a very noisy world. And we're not going to get a chance to get people to remember much about us. No company is. And so, we have to be really clear on what we want them to know about us. The way to do that is not to talk about speeds and feeds. It's not to talk about bits and mega-hertz. It's not to talk about why we are better than Windows.

The question we asked was, our customers want to know who is Apple and what is it that we stand for? Where do we fit in this world? What we're about isn't making boxes for people to get their jobs done, although we do that well. Apple's about something more than that. *Apple at the core, its core value is that we believe that people with passion can change the world for the better.* That's what we believe. And we believe that, in this world, people can change it for the better. And that those people who are crazy enough to think that they can change the world, are the ones that actually do. *Core values,* those things shouldn't change. The things that Apple believed in at its core are the same things that Apple really stands for today. It touches the soul of this company."

Rule #10: Stay Hungry, Stay Foolish

"Believe that things will work out. Follow your intuition and curiosity. Trust your heart even when it leads you off the well-worn path. You have to trust that the dots will somehow connect in your future. The only way to do great work is to love what you do. If you haven't found it yet, keep looking. *Don't settle. As with all matters of the heart, you'll know when you find it.*

Don't be trapped by living with the results of other people's thinking. Don't let the noise of others opinions drown out your own inner voice. And most important, have the courage to follow your heart and intuition. They somehow already know what you truly want to become. Everything else is secondary. *Stay hungry, stay foolish.*"

Steve Jobs Summary

1. Don't Live a Limited Life
2. Have Passion
3. Focus
4. Don't Sell Crap
5. Build a Great Team
6. Don't Do it for the Money
7. Be Proud of Your Products
8. Build Around Customers
9. Marketing is About Values
10. Stay Hungry, Stay Foolish

How can you apply these rules to your business or life today?

_____

_____

_____

_____

_____

_____

_____

_____

_____

_____

_____

#DidYouKnow: Steve Jobs briefly attended Reed College before dropping out and deciding to travel through India to seek enlightenment and study Zen Buddhism.

"You don't have to work on change. Change is automatic, but progress is not." –
Tony Robbins

- Motivational speaker and self-help author
- Provides fresh water to 100,000 people a day in India
- Author of six internationally bestselling books
- More than 4 million people have attended his live seminars
- Fortune Magazine named him the "CEO Whisperer"

Rule #1: Raise Your Standards *[Evan's Fav]*

"Ultimately, if you're going to have lasting change in anything, you're really talking about just raising your standards. Lasting change is different than a goal. *You don't always get your goals, but you always get your standards.* Most people have a list of 'shoulds.' When you decide something is a 'must' for you, an absolute 'must,' when you cut off any other possibility, you say, 'I'm going to find a way, or I'm going to make the way.'

Human beings, when they resolve things, when they make a real resolution inside themselves, they raise the standard and make it a 'must.' They find the way. I'd like to ask you to take a look at any place you've got a limitation and ask yourself, 'When did I decide to accept that limitation?' You may not even see it as a limitation. You might see it as, just, 'That's who I am.' So often in our lives, we've adapted to be a certain way, so that we don't fail or so that people will like us or respect us. It's not necessarily who we are. *We live who we believe we are.*"

Rule #2: Be Truly Fulfilled

"You've got to separate the vehicle from the outcome. What is it that's going to truly fulfill you? What is it that's going to give you that extraordinary life? What's going to make things magnificent, on your terms, not somebody else's terms, not your father, your mother, your background? What is that, really? Separate the vehicle. There are many ways to get to that vehicle. Sometimes you have to reevaluate what's going to really make you fulfilled. *What is your gift?* Are you an artist? Are you the talent that can produce something no one else produces? Are you an extraordinary entrepreneur that can take that gigantic gut-load of risk, create the vision, attract the talent that you need, the managers and leaders?

You may have all these abilities, but which one really fulfills you the most is going to be the critical question. We tend to want to do them all. You say, 'Well, I can do all these.' Yes, you can, but what will it do to your quality of life? See, again, the secret is going to be this: *What is an extraordinary life, on your terms, today?*"

Rule #3: Progress Equals Happiness

"Getting things is not going to make you happy. It doesn't matter what you get. All those things **might excite you for the moment.** Even a relationship, as magnificent as it may be, might be exciting for a while, but if you don't keep growing, that relationship isn't going to stay exciting.

Progress equals happiness, and if we can make progress on a regular basis, we feel alive. That's why, at the beginning of the year, we get this thing like, 'Okay. I could have this fresh start. I could really do what my soul desires. I could expand. I could grow. I could improve. I could change. Or maybe, better than change, I could progress.'

The economy is going to change, no matter what you want it to do. The weather is going to change. Relationships are going to change. Everything in life is always changing. We don't have to work on change. **Change is automatic, but progress is not.** If you want to make real progress, then you really have to look at your life in a different way. You have to say, I have to take control of this process and not just hope it's going to work out, like people do who make a resolution."

Rule #4: Love Your Customer

"Treat people, at the end of the relationship, like it's the beginning, and there won't be an end. That's not just your intimate relationship. What if you fell in love with your customers, with your clients more than your product, more than your company? If your entire life is about meeting their needs. If you loved your customers and clients you'd do anything. Guess what? They're going to love you. You want clients for life, not just customers.

Fall in love with them. Most people love their customers and clients as long as they buy from them, do what they want, respond to them. If they don't, they go, 'That's the end.' You want clients for life, not just customers. Fall in love with them. It's a different focus. It's a different meaning, and that creates a different life because you make decisions differently from that place."

Rule #5: Add Value

"What does it take to create world-class marketing? What is the unique selling proposition? What is what we *call 'value-added marketing,'* VAM? Today, most people are sick and tired of advertising because where is it? Everywhere.

I have a question for you. How many of you do not even see banner ads, anymore? Literally, it's there, but you don't perceive it. *Your brain literally washes it out.* 98% of the people wash it out, so don't buy them, unless you're going to create something really unique. It's a total waste of your money and your time, in the world we're in today.

Today, what creates marketing is when *you don't just market, but you add value to people.* You do something. You teach them. You give them an insight. You give something valuable that costs them nothing, and then they look to you as an expert. They look to you as a person that adds value. They want you to supply them more information, more experience, more products and more services."

Rule #6: Have an Exit Strategy

"If you lend me this whole business about meeting your needs, you can run a successful business, but it'll be a job because you'll never be able to sell it. If it's just meeting your needs, it's not a system. It demands your attention, your connection. It's giving what you want. Ultimately, it's not going to give somebody else what they want, so you can't sell it.

If you can't sell your business, if you don't have an exit strategy, you have a job. That doesn't mean you have to sell the business, but one of the most important decisions you make in business is, ultimately, if I was going to sell this, if I chose to, I have to know who would I sell this to. Most people don't have a clear exit strategy. They think, 'I'll come up with that someday.'

You have to start with that in mind. That has to be part of your focus, if you're going to be successful in your business."

Rule #7: Be Resourceful

"Whenever people fail to achieve their goals, 99.9% of the time, you ask them why and they'll tell you it's because of a lack of resources. That's what all these things are. 'I didn't have the support. I didn't have the money. We didn't have the time. We didn't have this. We didn't have that.' There is a resource that people believe is missing, and that resource belief structure then keeps people from ever being able to really lead because what leaders do is they find a way to maximize whatever resources they have, as little as they may be. They don't believe in limited resources. Resources are interesting, but the ultimate resources are the feelings of emotion that make you resourceful. Think of it this way: *Resourcefulness is the ultimate resource.* How many have had an idea, for example. It was a great idea. You're excited about it, and then you didn't do anything? Then, one day, there you saw it, on the shelf. You saw it somewhere. Someone stole your idea. How many have had this happen? The only difference between you and that person was not that they had more resources. They were more resourceful."

Rule #8: Pay Attention to the Little Things

"Success and failure are not giant events. You don't just suddenly become successful or suddenly have this cataclysmic event that makes you fail. It may look that way, *but failure comes from all the little things.* It's failure to make the call. It's failure to check the books. It's failure to say 'I'm sorry.' It's failure to push yourself to do things, physically, that you don't want to do. All those little failures, day after day, come together until, one day, some cataclysmic event happens, and you blame that. That event happened because you missed all the little stuff. *Success, by the way, is not some overnight event. It's all these little things.* Success is having a vision. Success is making it compelling. Success is really seeing it and feeling it, every day, with strong enough reasons. Success is feeling the sense that I'm here to grow, and I'm here to give something to the world, more than just myself. All the little stuff, that's where success comes from. In business, it comes from delivering more than anybody could imagine. All those things add up, and people go, 'Wow. That's who I want to do business with.'"

Rule #9: Look for Leverage

"Leverage is critical. You know how I get so much done? Because I don't just get it done. I know the outcome. I know the purpose, and I look for leverage. **Leverage is different than delegation.** What's the problem with delegation? Delegation is you have all that needs to be done, so you give it to someone else. You tell them what needs to be done, and when they don't do it, you're pissed off.

Leverage says, **'I can move the biggest boulder in the world, with a little bit of effort.** I have something I can do it with, but I'm still part of it.' Leverage is, 'If I'm going to leverage something here with Tom, I'm going to make sure Tom understands the what? The outcome. I want to make sure Tom understands the purpose, the why and the action.'

If I'm really productive, my productivity should enhance the world. If there's anything you hate to do, it's because you're either ineffective at it or you don't think it's very important, but it is urgent. You need to hire somebody for those things, and ideally, somebody who loves that job. You're never going to grow when your time is eaten up for activities that aren't that important. **Activity without high levels of purpose is the drain of your fortune.** Do it now. If you can't get it all now, do a part of it now. Leverage is power. Leverage is ultimate power."

Rule #10: Change Your Mindset

"How many of you have things, when you want to go achieve them, and this part of your voice goes, 'It's not going to happen' or 'Forget it'? How many have a voice that sometimes interrupts that good pattern? I was driving a 1968 Volkswagen that I had earned at $40 a week, as a janitor. **I had to change my mindset.** I'd say, 'Wealth is circulating in my life. Wealth flows to me, in avalanches of abundance. All my needs, desires and goals are met instantly by infinite intelligence.' I would imagine the abundance in my life, and I would feel so grateful. A year later, I went from making $38,000 a year to making a million dollars a year. In one year."

Tony Robbins Summary

1. Raise Your Standards
2. Be Truly Fulfilled
3. Progress Equals Happiness
4. Love Your Customers
5. Add Value
6. Have an Exit Strategy
7. Be Resourceful
8. Pay Attention to the Little Things
9. Look for Leverage
10.   Change Your Mindset

How can you apply these rules to your business or life today?

_____

_____

_____

_____

_____

_____

_____

_____

_____

_____

_____

#DidYouKnow: Tony Robbins uses cryotherapy to help his body recover from being on stage all day.

"It's not about outdoing anyone. It's about how to outdo yourself. You are your competition." – Simon Sinek

- Author and speaker on leadership and management
- Known for popularizing the concept of "Start With Why"
- His TEDx Talk is the 3rd most viewed video on TED.com
- Board member of Danspace Project to advance art and dance
- Has a B.A. in cultural anthropology from Brandeis University

Rule #1: Break the Rules

"You don't have to do it the way everybody else has done it. You can do it your way, you can break the rules, *you just can't get in the way of somebody else getting what they want.* That's rule number one."

Rule #2: Train Your Mind

"I was watching the Olympics and I was amazed at how bad the questions were that the reporters would ask all the athletes, 'Were you *nervous?*' And to a T, all the athletes went, 'No.'

What I realized is it's not that they're not nervous, it's their interpretation of what's happening in their bodies. What happens when you're nervous? Your heart rate starts to go. You sort of get a little tense. You get a little sweaty. You have expectation of what's coming and we interpret that as, 'I'm nervous.'

Now what's the interpretation of *excited?* Your heart rate starts to go. You're anticipating what's coming. You get a little tense. It's all the same thing, it's the same stimuli. Except these athletes, these Olympic quality athletes have learned to interpret the stimuli that the rest of us would say is 'nervous' as 'excited' They all said the same thing, 'No, I'm not nervous, I'm excited.'

I've actually practiced it just to tell myself when I start to get nervous, that this is excitement. I used to speak in front of a large audience, and somebody would say, 'How do you feel?' I used to say, 'A little nervous.' Now when somebody says, 'How do you feel?' I'm like, 'Pretty excited, actually!'

It came from telling myself, 'No, no, no, this is excitement,' and *it becomes a little bit automatic later on.*

It's a remarkable thing, to *deal with pressure by interpreting what your body is experiencing as excitement rather than nerves.* And it's really effective. It makes you want to rush forward rather than pull back, and yet it's the same experience."

Rule #3: Be Patient

"I talk to so many smart, fantastic, ambitious, idealistic, hardworking kids, and they're right out of college, they're in their entry-level jobs, and I'll ask them, 'How's it going?' And they'll say, 'I think I'm going to quit.' And I'm like, 'Why?' And they say to me, 'I'm not making an impact.' I'm like, 'You know you've been here eight months, right?'

But the problem is the sense of impatience. It's as if an entire generation is standing at the foot of a mountain. They know exactly what they want. **They can see the summit. What they can't see is the mountain.** This large, immovable object.

That doesn't mean you have to do your time. That's not what I'm talking about. Take a helicopter, climb, I don't care, but there's still a mountain. **Life, career fulfillment, relationships, are journeys.**

The problem is, this entire generation has an institutionalized sense of impatience, and do they have the patience to go on the journey to maintain love, **to feel fulfilled, or do they just quit, and on to the next?** Dump, and on to the next?"

Rule #4: Take Accountability

"Sometimes, you're the problem. We've seen this happen all too recently with our new men of science and empirical studiers, and these men of finance, who are smarter than the rest of us until the thing collapsed.

And they blamed everything else except themselves. And my point is, **take accountability for your actions.**

You can take all the credit in the world for the things that you do right, as long as you also take responsibility for the things you do wrong. **It must be a balanced equation.**

You don't get it one way and not the other. You get to take credit when you also take accountability."

Rule #5: Outdo Yourself

"Finite players play to beat the people around them. Infinite players play to be better than themselves. To wake up every single day and say, 'How can we make our company a better version of itself today than it was yesterday? How can we create a product this week that's better than the product we created last week?'

We also have to play the infinite game. It's not about being ranked number one. It's not about having more followers on Twitter than your friends. It's not about outdoing anyone. It's about how to outdo yourself. It's not about selling more books or getting more TED views than somebody else. *It's about how to make sure that the work that you're producing is better than the work you produced before.*

You are your competition. And that is what ensures you stay in the game the longest, and that is what ensures you find joy. Because the *joy comes not from comparison, but from advancement."*

Rule #6: Stack the Deck *[Evan's Fav]*

"When are you at your best? I'm at my best when I'm around people who believe what I believe. I know it seems silly, but I try very, very hard to stack the deck. *To put myself in a position of strength.*

So for example somebody asked me just yesterday, 'Have you ever had a bad engagement?' And I was thinking to myself, 'Not really.' But it's not because I'm some sort of genius or anything. It's because I stack the deck. It's because I want to be there. *I want to be around people who want me there.*

In other words, if I'm somebody's 10th choice, I'll probably turn it down. Whereas if I'm their first choice, they really want me there and so I'm more likely to have a good engagement. They're supportive of me and I'm supportive of them. I'm at my best when I stack the deck. *When I choose to be in an environment where my strengths are there."*

Rule #7: Be the Last to Speak

"You will be told your whole life that you need to learn to listen. I would say that you need to learn to be the last to speak. Even people who consider themselves good leaders will walk into a room and say, 'Here's the problem. Here's what I think. But I'm interested in your opinion. Let's go around the room.' It's too late. The skill to hold your opinions to yourself until everyone has spoken does two things. One, it gives everybody else the feeling that they have been heard. It gives everyone else the ability to feel that they have contributed. And two, you get the **benefit of hearing what everybody else has to think before you render your opinion.** The skill is really to keep your opinions to yourself. If you agree with somebody, don't nod yes. If you disagree with somebody, don't nod no. The only thing you're allowed to do is ask questions so that you can understand what they mean and why they have the opinion that they have. You must understand from where they are speaking. Why they have the opinion they have, not just what they are saying. And at the end, you will get your turn. It sounds easy, it's not. Practice being the last to speak."

Rule #8: Be Authentic

"Every decision we make in our lives, it's our way of saying something about who we are and what we believe. This is why authenticity matters. This is why you have to say and do the things you actually believe. **Because the things you say and do are symbols of who you are.** And we look for those symbols so we can find people who believe what we believe. So if you're putting out false symbols, you will attract people to those symbols. The companies that are crystal clear on what they believe and they're consistent in what they do, and everything they say, and everything they do serves as a symbol of the set of values and beliefs. We use those symbols to say something about who we are. We surround ourselves with the people and the products, and the brands, that say something about who we are. And when we can find the people who believe what we believe, we're weirdly drawn to them. And so the more you can give of yourself, the more you can give of what you believe, the more you can discipline, say and do the things you actually believe, strange things start to happen."

Rule #9: Find Your Passion

"Passion is the feeling you have that you would probably do this for free and you can't believe somebody pays you to do it. I think we mistake that passion is something we do in our private lives but it shouldn't be done in our careers. I'm a firm believer that you are who you are and anybody who says, 'I'm different at home than I am at work,' you're lying. The goal is to make everything you do, at home and at work, something that you have excitement to do. So how do you find the things that you're excited to do? Well it's actually easier than you think. What are the things that you love to do? What are the things that you would do for free? How can you recreate that feeling, and get paid for it? What are the things that I do on the weekend?"

Rule #10: Start with Why

"How do you explain when others are able to achieve things that seem to defy all of the assumptions? *Why, how, what.* This little idea explains why some organizations, and some leaders, are able to inspire where others aren't. Every single organization on the planet knows what they do. Some know how they do it, whether you call it your differentiating value proposition, or your USP, but very, very few people or organizations know why they do what they do. And by why I don't mean to make a profit. That's a result. By why, I mean *what's your purpose? What's your cause?* What's your belief? Why does your organization exist? Why do you get out of bed in the morning? And why should anyone care? The inspired leaders and the inspired organizations, regardless of their size, regardless of their industry, all think, act, and communicate from the inside out. People don't buy what you do, they buy why you do it. The goal is not to do business with everybody who needs what you have, *the goal is to do business with people who believe what you believe.* Leaders hold a position of power but those who lead, inspire us. Whether they're individuals or organizations, we follow those who lead, not because we have to, but because we want to. We follow those who lead not for them, but for ourselves. And it's those who start with why that have the ability to inspire those around them, or find others who inspire them."

Simon Sinek Summary

1. Break the Rules
2. Train Your Mind
3. Be Patient
4. Take Accountability
5. Outdo Yourself
6. Stack the Deck
7. Be the Last to Speak
8. Be Authentic
9. Find Your Passion
10. Start with Why

How can you apply these rules to your business or life today?

_____

_____

_____

_____

_____

_____

_____

_____

_____

_____

_____

_____

#DidYouKnow: Simon Sinek is a trained ethnographer, one who studies people and cultures.

"Picking a partner is crucial. Somebody who you shares your vision and yet has a little bit different set of skills." – Bill Gates

- Entrepreneur, investor, author, and philanthropist
- Co-founded Microsoft in 1975
- Has given over $28 billion to charity
- Named one of the 100 who most influenced the 20th century
- Consistently ranks in the list of the world's wealthiest people

Rule #1: Overcome Your Fear of Risk

"When I started Microsoft, I didn't think of it as all that risky. I was so excited about what we were doing. It's true, I could've gone bankrupt, but I had a set of skills that were highly employable. And in fact, my parents were still willing to let me go back to Harvard and finish my education if I wanted to.

The thing that was scary to me wasn't quitting and starting the company, *it was when I started hiring my friends and they expected to be paid.* And then we had customers who went bankrupt, customers that I counted on to come through. Then I got this incredibly conservative approach that I wanted to have enough money in the bank to pay a year's worth of payroll, even if we didn't get any payments coming in.

If you are going to start a company, it takes so much energy that you better overcome your feeling of risk. If you're young, it's hard to go lease premises. They made that hard for me. You couldn't rent a car when you were under 25 at the time, so I was always taking taxis to go see customers, and people would say 'We're going to go and have a discussion in the bar,' but I couldn't go in the bar.

But that's fun, because when people are first skeptical and they know this kid doesn't know anything, then when you show them that you've really got a good product, and that you know something, they actually tend to go overboard and they think, 'Whoa, they know a lot! Let's really do an incredible amount with these people.' But those problems are common starting the firm. *You better think of those as part of the pleasure, part of the challenge that is part of the excitement."*

Rule #2: Always Be a Student

"I'm a weird dropout because I take college courses all the time. *I love learning. I love being a student.*

I feel it was unfortunate that I didn't get to stay there but I don't think I missed any knowledge because whatever I needed to learn, I was still in a learning mode."

Rule #3: Work Hard

"I'm in meetings a lot. My calendar gets very full. And then at night, after the kids have gone to bed, I'm on **email a great deal.** I get messages during the day, and that's my chance to give long responses.

Then over the weekend I send a lot of mails as well. **I take two weeks a year to just go off and read and think,** where I'm not interrupted by work or anything else.

I'm just solidly trying to think about the future, and people get to send me things to read as part of that so-called **think week.** So, it's a nice mix of things.

About 25% of the time that I'm out traveling around meeting with customers in Europe, Asia, and that sort of helps me think, 'Okay, do we have the **right priorities?** What are people responding well to? What would they like to see us do better?'"

Rule #4: Learn to Say No

"First I met Warren [Buffett].

We were talking about getting together and doing something again.

He pulled out his calendar, and the **pages were so blank.**

I said, 'Wow, you've managed to **avoid getting tied in to a lot of meaningless activity.'**

Warren said, 'Yeah, you have to **be good at saying no** and picking the things that really make a difference.'

That's one of many things I've learned from Warren, but that's one of my favorites so I can blame it on him whenever I'm turning things down."

Rule #5: Enjoy What You Do *[Evan's Fav]*

"The key point is: **You've got to enjoy what you do every day.**

And for me that's working with very smart people. It's working on new problems.

Every time we think 'Hey, we've had a little bit of success', we're pretty careful not to dwell on it too much because the bar gets raised."

Rule #6: Be Fanatical

"People who have been successful are often, not always, **pretty fanatical** about the thing they're trying to do.

I remember one industry panel where there were about seven people and the debate was would the computer interface be this character-mode thing or would it be graphic user interface?

At the time, the graphic user interface stuff was so slow it was laughable. Writing software for it was so bad. It was Windows 1.0.

The people on the panel were saying, 'No, no. This is kind of a stupid thing.'

I would say, 'No, believe me. This'll be great.' One of the guys on the panel said, 'Hey, Bill is wrong, but Bill works harder than the rest of us. **Even though it's the wrong solution, he's likely to succeed.'**

That was the best compliment I ever had.

Just by working day and night, I could send the industry in some direction. I was fanatical in that period of time, that is, I didn't believe in vacation. I didn't believe in weekends.

It turned out that worked for me that we got our company going at a speed that allowed it to **make mistakes faster** than other people were and see those mistakes."

Rule #7: Ask for Advice

"I've talked to my dad, I talk to Warren [Buffett], I talk to my wife Melinda.

I have enough people that know me, and actually know where my judgment isn't its strongest, where I might get over excited about something, or *forget to think about something.*

They're good at *correcting whatever those blind spots are.* And I think it's good to encourage your friends and advisors to really give them that license.

I can go to the party and forget to say hello to various people or something. That's a very minor example of my blind spots.

A small number of people that you can turn to on certain key things is a great asset."

Rule #8: Pick Good People

"My best business decisions really have to do with picking people. Deciding to go into partnership with Paul Allen is probably at the top of the list. And then, subsequently, hiring a friend, Steve Balmer.

Having somebody who you totally trust, who is totally committed, who *shares your vision and yet has a little bit different set of skills* and also acts as a check on you.

Some of the ideas you come up with you run by them, because you know they're going to say 'Hey, wait a minute, have you thought about this and that?'

Just the benefit *of sparking off with somebody* who's got that kind of brilliance, it's not only made it fun, but it's really led to a lot of success.

So, picking a partner is crucial."

Rule #9: Don't Procrastinate

"I had one habit that I developed when I was at college, that was actually a very bad habit, which was I liked to show people that I didn't do any work, and that I didn't go to classes, and I didn't care. And then, at the very last minute, like two days before the test, I'd get serious about it. And people thought that was funny. That was my positioning, the guy that did nothing until the last minute. Then when I went into business, that was a really bad habit, and it took me a couple years to get over that. Nobody praised me because I would do things at the last minute. I'm still working on it, but *procrastination is not a good habit.*"

Rule #10: Be Practical

"Even in the early days, if you said, 'A computer on every desk in every home', and you'd say, 'Okay, how many homes are there in the world? How many desks are there in the world? Can I make $20 for every home, $20 for every desk?' You could get these big numbers, but part of the beauty of the whole thing was we were very *focused on the here and now*. Should we hire one more person? If our customers didn't pay us, would we have enough cash to meet the payroll?

We really were very *practical* about that next thing and so involved in the deep engineering that we didn't get ahead of ourselves. We never thought how big we'd be. I remember when one of the early lists of wealthy people came out. One of the Intel founders was there. The guy who ran Wang Computer Factory was still doing well. We thought, 'If the software business does well, the value of Microsoft could be similar to that,' but it wasn't a real focus. The everyday activity of just doing great software drew us in. Some decisions we made, like the quality of the people and the vision of how we thought about software. That was very long-term. We just came into work every day, wrote more code, hired more people. It wasn't really until the IBM PC succeeded and perhaps even until Windows succeeded that there was a broad awareness that Microsoft was very unique as a software company and that these other companies had been *one-product companies.*"

Bill Gates Summary

1. Overcome Your Fear of Risk
2. Always Be a Student
3. Work Hard
4. Learn to Say No
5. Enjoy What You Do
6. Be Fanatical
7. Ask for Advice
8. Pick Good People
9. Don't Procrastinate
10. Be Practical

How can you apply these rules to your business or life today?

_____

_____

_____

_____

_____

_____

_____

_____

_____

_____

#DidYouKnow: Bill Gates reads 50 books a year, and once he starts a book, he has to finish it.

"What do you want? How much do you want to live? Stop just waking up like an accident." – Eric Thomas

- Motivational speaker, author and minister
- Lebron James credited him as part his inspiration for winning
- Was homeless for two years and ate from trash cans
- While homeless, a preacher inspired him to go back to school
- His speeches on YouTube helped him rise to prominence

Rule #1: Know What You Want

"You can't dangle something in front of my face. I don't want that. *Many of you aren't taking anything because you don't know what you want.*

If I can do one thing for you, I don't want nothing from you but for you to know what you want.

What do you want in your marriage? What do you want with your son and your daughter? What do you want in your health? What do you want financially? How much money do you want to make a year? What do you want to drive? How do you want to live? *Stop just waking up like an accident.*

What do you want? And then once you find out what you want, *spend the rest of your natural life waking up and going after it.* The reason why I speak with so much passion, 'E.T., why do you speak with so much authority?' Because I'm talking about my life. Not something that I read.

I ate out of trash cans. I had no business eating out of trash cans. I lived in abandoned buildings. I had no business living in abandoned buildings. 'But, E.T., your daddy wasn't in your life. Your mom was a teenage mother.' *There is no excuse for not living up to your fullest potential. No excuse."*

Rule #2: Work on Your Gift

"I worked on my gift. I realize that *all of us are born with a gift, but you've got to hone it.*

We talk about greatness is upon you and I realized that my gift wasn't going to create itself. *My gift wasn't going to nurture itself.* My gift wasn't going to perfect itself. That was something I had to do.

Man, before you know it we did a video that went viral. I think it's got over 50 million hits now and *we turned our passion into our profit."*

Rule #3: No Excuses *[Evan's Fav]*

"You know what's so funny? *We want people to make guarantees to us but we're not willing to make guarantees to ourselves.* Now like you, somebody gave you a guarantee, 30 day guarantee. In 30 days, if you don't make what they told you, you was going to make, in 30 days you got an attitude. You want your money back. But you never demanded your money back from yourself.

You've never looked at yourself in the mirror and said you let you down. Until you get to that point, you let you down. You're not brave enough. You want to put it on somebody else. The reason why I'm not successful is because of my boss. Have you ever looked at yourself in the mirror and said, 'I'm not getting up on time. I'm not going to work on time. I'm not putting in 120% when I'm at work. I let me down.'

You always want to blame other people. You want to hold other people to the fire but you're not holding yourself to the fire. You owe you an explanation. You need to look at yourself in the mirror and say, 'Why are you only giving 50%? What's wrong with you?' You need to put yourself in punishment. You need to tell you, 'No more TV, no more snacks, no more desserts, no more. No, we working out now.' I didn't get here making excuses. You need to get rid of them excuses and you need to stop pointing fingers at people. *And you need to start pointing fingers at yourself.* What did you not do?"

Rule #4: Upgrade Your Values

"Those of you that said I want to be a millionaire, I want to be the best at this company, right? But your value system says *you believe in sleep more than you believe in grinding.* Your value system says you are a consumer and not a producer. And you're spending more money than you're making.

Why? Because you're a consumer but you're reading all the books and you're saying everything the books are saying. But those books are not in alignment with your values. *If you're going to go to the next level, your values are going to have to change.*"

Rule #5: You Reap What You Sow

"I have 24 hours and they're mine. This 24 hours belongs to me and whatever I do in this 24 hours will **determine where I'll be tomorrow and the next day,** and I think that's what people need to focus on. Like get off of this, 'I want to make six figures. I want to drive this car. I want to live in this house.'

I think what people should be focusing on is, 'I have 24 hours. Oprah only has 24. Bill Gates only has 24. Warren Buffett only has 24 hours. And **in that 24 hour period, I can either break my life or make my life.'**

I think what should be on the priority list is going to bed, so you can wake up the next day and you can grind it out. I'm just a dude that believes you reap what you sow. So if you're grinding on Monday, grinding on Tuesday, grinding on Wednesday. **If you're grinding six, seven days a week for a span of five or six years, something's got to come out of that.**

If we would **spend more time on, 'What's my goal?',** meaning what do I need to accomplish in this day to live this lifestyle and you go after it, then I think more people will be successful."

Rule #6: Education is the Equalizer

"Education is the great equalizer. No matter where you are, if you feel like you started at the bottom and you're like, 'Man, I'm at the bottom Eric, and I want to live life like everybody else. I want to fly first class. I want to see the world. I don't want any limitations.'

I had to realize for myself, being a high school dropout. You can't use that excuse forever. Where I was born and where I was raised, you can't use that forever. So to me, you liberate yourself.

It's not optional. **The more you read, the more liberated you are** and the more you are educated the more you can experience life like the people you're probably looking at and saying, 'I wish I could live like that person.'"

Rule #7: What is Your Why?

"What's your why? Hey, if I don't give you all nothing else, you better start with *what's your why.* You know why I do what I do and I do it so passionately? Because my grandfather was a high school dropout. My father was a high school dropout. I was a high school dropout and we about to break the cycle.

I do what I do so my son won't have to go through what I went through. I do what I do because my daughter says she going to Harvard. *It ain't even about you.*

What's your why? *Why do you wake up in the morning?* Why do you put on that jersey? Why do you go out and practice? Why?"

Rule #8: Have Boundaries

"I have boundaries. So just because it's my company, it doesn't mean I can take calls all day. I have boundaries so you can't call me at a certain time. Why? I'm working. So I'm on the phone all day and I'm saying this to entrepreneurs because one of the gaps for entrepreneurs is that they feel like because they own their day, they can spend it like they want. You cannot spend it like you want to. So if you were working for IBM or you were working for Ford, whoever you were working for, you couldn't be on the phone all day at a major corporation. So why do you allow yourself to talk on the phone when you're a business?

One of my rituals is when I get started, there are no interruptions. When I get started, I don't care if it's my wife, my children, they know that for a certain time frame, I'm going all in and I can't go all in and answer the phone. I can't go all in watching TV. I can't go in with the distraction. Some entrepreneurs are like, 'Why am I not blowing up?' You don't have that moment of your day. I don't care if it's two hours, four hours, where you *shut the entire world out.* No Twitter. No Facebook. No nothing. No Instagram. We love that Instagram. Your content probably will be stronger if you had that time of isolation, of solitude, where you give yourself a chance to think, you give yourself a chance to go in. And when you go in, you go 120%."

Rule #9: Speak From the Heart

"I think what's so unique about my presentation is that it comes from the heart. *I speak from the heart and I'm not afraid to be transparent.* I'm not afraid to talk about my failures. I'm not afraid to talk about my fears. I'm not afraid to open up my life and give my story to the world."

Rule #10: Succeed as Bad as You Want to Breathe

"So if you want to make six figures, you can't just be talking about you want to make six figures. *When you want to succeed as bad as you want to breathe, then you'll be successful.* I don't know how many of you all got asthma but if you've ever had an asthma attack before, the only thing you trying to do is get some air. You don't care about no basketball game. You don't care what's on TV. You don't care about nobody calling you. You don't care about a party. The only thing you care about is to get some fresh air. That's it. And when you get to the point where all you want to do is be successful as bad as you want to breathe, then you'll be successful. And I'm here to tell you, number one, that most of you say you want to be successful but you don't want it bad.

You just kind of want it. You don't want it badder than you want to party. You don't want it as much as you want to be cool. Most of you don't want success as much as you want to sleep. Some of you love sleep more than you love success. And I'm here to tell you today, *if you're going to be successful, you've got to be willing to give up sleep.* You've got to be willing to work off three hours of sleep, two hours. If you really want to be successful, some days you going to have to stay up three days in a row. *Because if you go to sleep, you might miss the opportunity to be successful.* That's how bad you've got to want it. Listen to me. You've got to want to be successful so bad that you forget to eat. I'll never forget, when 50 Cent was doing his movie, I did a little research on 50. And 50 said that when he wasn't doing the movie, he was doing the sound track. And they said, 'When do you sleep, 50?' He says, 'Sleep? Sleep is for those people who are broke. I don't sleep.'"

Eric Thomas Summary

1. Know What you Want
2. Work on Your Gift
3. No Excuses
4. Upgrade Your Values
5. You Reap What You Sow
6. Education is the Equalizer
7. What is Your "Why"?
8. Have Boundaries
9. Speak from the Heart
10. Succeed as Bad as You Want to Breathe

How can you apply these rules to your business or life today?

_____

_____

_____

_____

_____

_____

_____

_____

_____

_____

#DidYouKnow: Eric Thomas spent 12 years working toward an undergraduate degree and graduated in 2001.

"How your experience of life is on this planet is 100% determined by you if you take charge of this." - Sadhguru

- Yogi, mystic, philanthropist and author
- Was voted among the 100 most powerful Indians
- Recognized for his contribution to environmental protection
- Spoke at United Nations Millennium World Peace Summit
- His book, 'Inner Engineering' is a New York Times bestseller

Rule #1: Enhance Your Perception

"Effort has to be incisive in a sense. It should be focused, calibrated. Simply if you make effort, it's foolish effort, isn't it? Just labor is not going to get you somewhere. The right kind of action, the right timing, right place. All this is important, isn't it? So for all these things to happen, you need **perception and intelligence.** So that's all you must do in your life. Constantly looking for ways to enhance your perception and your intelligence. The rest will happen anyway. This is one thing that, unfortunately, humanity is not doing. They're trying to become capable of something. Just enhance your perception and intelligence."

Rule #2: Take Charge of Your Life

"Can you see me right now, all of you? Can you see me? Just point out where I am. Use your hands and point out. Can you see me? Oh you got it wrong. You know I am a mystic. You're getting it completely wrong. Now this light is falling upon me, reflecting, going through your lenses, in order to imagine you're 80 now. You know the whole story, right? Where do you see me right now? **Within yourself.** Where do you hear me right now? Within yourself. Where have you seen the whole world? Within yourself.

Have you ever experienced anything outside of yourself? Everything that ever happened to you. Darkness and light happened within you. Pain and pleasure happened within you. Joy and misery happened within you. Have you ever experienced anything outside of yourself? No, so what I am asking you is what happens within you? Who should determine how it should happen? Somebody else? **Definitely you should determine what should happen within.**

So if you determine what's happening within this, your whole experience of life will be determined by you. Nobody else but you. The events around you may not be determined by you, but how **your experience of life is on this planet is 100% determined by you** if you take charge of this. If you leave it loose, just about anybody will determine it. They will. Not consciously. They also, like you, by accident."

38

Rule #3: Be Conscious of Your Mortality

"If you just observe, if everybody makes a little effort, everybody take a little time for this piece of life. Not for your family. Not for your career. Not for something else. *Just for this piece of life.* Give it little time because this is the most important piece of life in your life. Even if you are in love with somebody. Still, this is their most important piece of life. So pay some attention to this. How does it happen? Why have you taken it for granted? Believe me, you're not going to be here forever. I will bless you with a long life, but you are going to fall dead one day.

So do not take this for granted. If you wake up in the morning, tomorrow, it is not my wish, but I want you to know, of all the people who go to bed tonight, over a million people will not wake up tomorrow morning. And if you and me wake up tomorrow morning, is it not a fantastic thing? A million people did not wake up. You woke up. Is that not a great thing? That is all that is needed. *If you want to know the value of life, just know that it's a brief happening."*

Rule #4: Take a Holiday From Seriousness

"Loosen up your life a little bit, laugh a little more, involve yourself with people around you. Do things that you think is not so important. Don't do things which are very important. Do simple things. It's very important you do simple things. Very important things you are doing in your life, you will become very serious. Bertrand Russell said *if you're beginning to think that what you're doing is very important, you need to take a holiday.* So holiday does not mean coming to India. Holiday is every day. In those 24 hours, you must take a holiday from your seriousness, from yourself. Seriousness comes essentially because of your self-importance. You hold yourself as an important person. I want you to see you are like a speck of dust in this existence.

Tomorrow morning if you disappear, the world will go on fine without you, whoever you may be. Isn't it so? If you constantly remind yourself of this, you will have no reason to be serious. Don't be dead now. The time will come. *It's time to be alive."*

39

Rule #5: Produce Nice Movies in Your Mind

"To create fear, you have to use excessive imagination. To not be in fear, you don't have to do anything. Fear is happening because of excessive imagination. Things that have not happened, you are creating. What may happen in your mind happens in a thousand different formats. And most probably never happen. *The things that you fear, probably 99 of them never happened.*

Fear means you are producing horror movies in your mind nobody else is willing to watch. That's bad for the producer. But you're producing them. So you produce something else. Produce a comedy, a love story, suspense, thriller. Try and see, today. Just sit down and produce a love story, a suspense thriller, a comedy. Five-minute movies you make in your mind. *Really, start using your mind differently.*"

Rule #6: Don't Identify with Anything

"The nature of the human being is such. No matter what you do, *you want to be something more than what you are right now.* If that something more happens, something more, something more, it's an endless pursuit. So somewhere, a human being is seeking a limitless expansion but trying to do it with physical means. The very nature of physicality is a defined boundary. If there is no defined boundary, there is no possibility of physical happening in the universe.

But now a human being is longing for the boundless. That too in installments, and through physical means. Through the boundary, you are trying to become boundless. The desire is fantastic. The method is hopeless. Because *the moment you identify yourself with something, your intellect's work is just to protect that identity.* Whatever identities of nation or family or gender or race, religion. The moment you identify yourself with something, your intellect will only function around that to protect that, so it is a certain type of prejudice the moment you identify. So the only thing I did with my life is, I never identified myself with anything. And life just exploded within me, in ways that thought seemed so puny that I do not indulge in thought most of the time."

Rule #7: Fix Yourself *[Evan's Fav]*

"Pleasantness is a choice. So why is it so much unpleasantness is happening? Because we never took charge of the inner damage. We believe by fixing the outside everything is going to be okay. In the last 150 years, with the advent of science and technology, we have fixed too many things on the outside. If you fix any more, there won't be a planet left. I know you have series of complaints about how things are not okay, but we are the most comfortable generation ever before on this planet. But we cannot say we are the most joyful generation on the planet. We are the most loving generation on the planet. We are the most blissed-out generation on the planet. Definitely not. We are complaining like crazy about everything like never before. This is because we fixed the outside. *Comfort and convenience has happened. Wellbeing has not happened.* If your interiority was handled by you consciously, you would definitely keep this in a blissful state. So is bliss the goal of life? No, bliss is a necessary condition for life to flower to its full potential. Otherwise, it will remain constrained."

Rule #8: Your Happiness Comes from You

"You're paying too much attention to everything around you, not enough attention to this one. But the quality of your life is essentially determined by how you carry this one, isn't it so? This moment, what kind of coat you're wearing, what kind of car you parked outside, what kind of home you live in does not determine the quality of your life. This moment, how joyful are you feeling within yourself determines the quality of your life, yes or no? Nothing has been done about it. You think it will happen in consequence, and you're setting impossible goals for your happiness. If I have to be happy, my wife should be like this, my husband should be like that, my children should be like this, the world should become some other way. Well, these are impossible conditions you are setting for your happiness and peacefulness. To be peacefully essentially means this: That you are not messing your mind. *To be peaceful means that your system is at ease.* You know how to conduct your mind. You know how to conduct your emotions, your body, and your energies. You are peaceful. It is not a rocket technology. It is the most basic thing."

Rule #9: Don't Set Incentives for Sickness

"Unfortunately, in many ways 70% of illnesses on the planet, all kinds, are self-created. *If you keep yourself in a certain way physically and mentally, the virus and the bacteria will not work* in the same way as it works upon somebody else. The last 29 years, I have not been able to cancel one program because I am running a temperature, I got a cold, I got this, I got that. It doesn't matter what's happening. What you have to do, you anyway have to do.

If it's summer, you still go, right? No a lot of people don't go. It's a little hot outside, they don't go and work. A little cold outside, they don't go and work. A little raining and they won't go and work. A snowflake, they will not go and work. This is just weather. So for every change in weather, if you have the comfort of covering yourself in a blanket and lying down, once you create that, your body will learn to fall sick as often as possible. If you just keep it this way, it doesn't matter what it is, anyway I have to go and do what I have to do, you will see your body will just bounce back as quickly as possible, even if it gets the worst kind of infections.

So you just *have to set the necessary conditions for health*, both for yourself and your children if you have them. Do not set incentives for sickness."

Rule #10: Always Do Your Best

"When the result of the event has no impact on you. Both ways you're blissed out. You're a success. *When the fruit of the action does not determine how you are.* You do things because of the exuberance of what you do, then you are a success. The result may depend on variety of things. Results are not always yours.

For any result to happen, whether it's in a game or in life situations, there are various factors involved. Not all of it is in our control. But what is in our control is either we did our best or we did not do our best. That's in our control. As long as we're doing that, and whatever the result may be, if you're still blissed out that means you are a success because *life cannot defeat you anymore.*"

Sadhguru Summary

1. Enhance Your Perception
2. Take Charge of Your Life
3. Be Conscious of Mortality
4. Take a Holiday from Seriousness
5. Produce Nice Movies
6. Don't Identify with Anything
7. Fix Yourself
8. Your Happiness Comes from You
9. Don't Set Incentives for Sickness
10. Always Do Your Best

How can you apply these rules to your business or life today?

_____

_____

_____

_____

_____

_____

_____

_____

_____

_____

#DidYouKnow: Sadhguru created the Isha Insight program in order to help small and medium businesses scale up.

"Three things in hiring people: Look for integrity, intelligence, and energy." – Warren Buffett

- Was the single most successful investor of the 20th century
- Has been Chairman of Berkshire Hathaway since 1970
- Time named him one of the most influential people globally
- Believes in value investing and personal frugality
- Pledged to give away 99% of his fortune to charities

Rule #1: Find Your Passion *[Evan's Fav]*

"Find your passion.

I was very, very lucky to find it when I was seven or eight years old, and, fortunately, my children have found their passion.

One son loves farming like nothing else. One son loves music like everything else.

And all three of them love philanthropy and what they get to do.

You are lucky in life when you find it and you can't guarantee that you are going to find it at your first job.

I always tell college students, *'Take the job you would take if you were independently wealthy. You are going to do well at it.'*

If you think you are going to be a lot happier if you have 2x instead of x you are probably making a mistake.

You've got to find something you like that works with that and *you will get in trouble if you think that making 10x or 20x is the answer* for everything in life because then you will do things like borrow money when you shouldn't or cut corners on things that your employer wants you to cut corners on.

It just doesn't make any sense and you won't like it when you look back on it."

Rule #2: Hire Well

"Three things in hiring people: Look for integrity, intelligence and energy.

If a person doesn't have the first one, the latter two will kill them, because if they don't have integrity, you want them dumb and lazy. You don't want them smart and energetic."

Rule #3: Don't Care What Others Think

"It never bothers me if people disagree with what I thought, as long as I felt I knew the facts.

There is a whole bunch of things I don't know a thing about.

I just stay away from those.

So I stay within what I call my *circle of competence.*

Tom Watson said it best. He said, 'I'm no genius, but I'm smart in spots, and I stay around those spots.'

Well I try and stay around those spots, and I just don't have a problem if somebody says, 'You are wrong' on something.

I just go back and look at the facts.

I think that really is much more important, frankly, than having a few points of IQ or having an extra course or two in school.

You need emotional stability."

Rule #4: Read, Read, Read

*"*I just *read, and read, and read.*

I probably read five to six hours a day.

I don't read as fast now as when I was younger, but I read five daily newspapers.

I read a fair number of magazines. I read 10- K's. I read annual reports and I read a lot of other things too.

I've always enjoyed reading.

I love reading biographies."

Rule #5: Have a Margin of Safety

"Famous lesson about a margin of safety: You don't drive a truck that weighs 9,000 pounds across the bridge that says limit 10,000 pounds because you can't be that sure about it.

If you see something like that, you go further down the road and you find the one that says limit 20,000 pounds and that's the one you cross."

Rule #6: Have a Competitive Advantage

"The nature of capitalism is that people want to come in and take your castle. It's perfectly understandable.

If I'm selling television sets, there's going to be 10 other people who are going to try to sell a better television set.

If I have a restaurant down here in Omaha, people are going to try and copy my menu and give more parking.

And take my chef and so on.

So, capitalism is all about somebody coming in trying to take the castle.

Now, what you need is a castle that has some durable competitive advantage. Some castle that has a moat around it. One of the best moats in many respects is to be a low cost producer.

But sometimes the moat is *just having more talent.*

I mean, if you're the heavyweight champion of the world and you keep knocking out people you've got competitive advantage as long as you can keep doing it.

And it's very profitable if you're the one that happens to be able to do it."

Rule #7: Schedule for Your Personality

"You'd be surprised at my days. They are very unstructured. No meetings. *I don't like meetings.* I read a lot. I wish I were a faster reader. I'd get more done. But I do read a lot. And I'm on the phone a moderate amount.

Our businesses run themselves basically. *My job is allocating capital* and that's what I'm thinking about. But I don't like to have things all packed hour to hour to hour.

Bill (Gates) and I are both extraordinarily lucky. I mean we really get to do what we like to do, the way we want to do it, with people that we choose to be around *and that are terrific.* I mean, we've really got everything our way, and we're very fortunate.

And in his world he has a different kind of pace than I have, but we both love it the way we do it and my guess is that we're each the most productive in that particular mode. *It fits our personalities and aptitudes.*"

Rule #8: Always Be Competing

"What kills great businesses, if you look at, and I do believe in looking at history and I like to study failure actually, and then my partner says, 'All I want to know is where I'll die so I'll never go there,' and we want to see what has caused businesses to go bad. *The biggest thing that kills them is complacency.*

You want a restlessness, a feeling that somebody's always after you, but you're going to stay ahead of them. You always want to be on the move.

And when you've got a great business, like Coca-Cola, the danger would always be that you rest on your laurels but I see none of that obviously at Coca-Cola. But that is the key, to compete the same way when you've got 1.8 billion servings being sold daily as when you were selling 10 a day, and *that restlessness, that belief that tomorrow's more exciting than today.* You just have to have it permeate the organization."

Rule #9: Model Success

"[Ben Graham'] was a wonderful man and he was my professor at Columbia.

I read his book when I was nineteen at the University in Nebraska. *I started investing when I was 11.*

I started reading about it when I was seven, so I've gone through it all. I read every book in the Omaha public library by the time I was twelve on investing and the stock market.

And I had a lot of fun, but I never really found out, I never got grounded in anything, and it was entertaining but it wasn't going to be profitable. And then I read Graham's book, 'The Intelligent Investor,' when I was at University of Nebraska. That just opened the whole thing up to me.

Ben Graham in his low teens looked around and he looked at the people he admired and he said, 'I want to be admired, so why don't I just behave like them?'

And he found that *there is nothing impossible about behaving like them."*

Rule #10: Give Unconditional Love

"The biggest lesson I got is the power of unconditional love, I think there's no power on Earth like unconditional love.

I think that you offer that to your child, and you are 90% of the way home.

To know that you can always come back, that is huge in life. That takes you a long, long way.

And I would say that *every parent out there that can extend that to their child* at a very young age, that's going to make for a better human being."

Warren Buffett Summary

1. Find Your Passion
2. Hire Well
3. Don't Care What Others Think
4. Read, Read, Read
5. Have a Margin of Safety
6. Have a Competitive Advantage
7. Schedule for Your Personality
8. Always Be Competing
9. Model Success
10. Give Unconditional Love

How can you apply these rules to your business or life today?

_____

_____

_____

_____

_____

_____

_____

_____

_____

_____

#DidYouKnow: Warren Buffett loves playing bridge and spends 12 hours a week playing the game, sometimes with his good friend Bill Gates.

"What FOCUS stands for is this: Follow One Course Until you're Successful." – *Robert Kiyosaki*

- Businessman, investor, author, and motivational speaker
- Author of the best-selling "Rich Dad, Poor Dad" series.
- Challenged the way millions of people think about money
- Believes that financial literacy should be taught in schools
- Served as a helicopter gunship pilot during the Vietnam War

Rule #1: Experience Makes You Smarter

"The last thing I want to talk about, debt, is one of the best investments I've made because I started off with no money, like most people. My first investment was a little $18,000 condo in Hawaii and I made a whopping $25 a month.

I didn't make much money on that deal, but every time I did an investment, be it real estate or business, *I got smarter because experience makes you smarter.* I started with just a little $18,000 unit. I broke out my credit card.

I paid the $2,000 down payment with my credit card, so it was 100% financed. Now, most experts will tell you, 'That's stupid. You don't do that,' but if you know what you're doing, you can do it.

A number of years ago, I bought a $7 million commercial building. I paid for it with zero down. Every month, after everything is paid for, it puts about $30,000 a month income in my pocket, or $360,000 a year for no money down. There is a price of having a good education or a bad education. *A good education is knowing the good debt versus bad debt* and how debtors can win, if you know what you're doing."

Rule #2: Give More, Receive More *[Evan's Fav]*

"I don't know what the heck people think about money, but that's what I get a lot of, is this, 'Well, money is not spiritual.' I'm just saying it's your attitudes, a person's attitude towards money.

I make a lot of money, but I give a lot. It goes to biblical principles. *The more you give, the more you receive.* When I meet somebody who doesn't have any money, it just means that they're not giving something. A lot of times, there are people who would like more, but they're not giving anything. They're like my poor dad. He belonged to the labor unions, and he wanted to work less and get paid more. That's anti-religious to me. *If you want to get paid more, work more, give more. That's how I see it.*"

Rule #3: Change the Way You Think

"The discipline I had to get into was I was paying myself first, even when I had no money, and when I have all these bill collectors calling me, I used them as inspiration. When the government's hounding you, the bill collectors are calling, because I've been broke, so I can understand what it feels like to be broke. When those guys are calling you, instead of shrinking, going into the shell, *I used it as motivation to go out and make more money.* I used my bill collectors as motivation, and that's why I paid myself first. I always bought assets. I'd buy a house, or I'd put money in the bank, because we are our biggest asset. We are also our biggest liability."

Rule #4: Focus

"The common wisdom, the old intelligence idea, is to diversify. What I believe in is something else. It's increase your financial IQ, your financial intelligence and, instead, FOCUS. What FOCUS stands for is this: *FOCUS is Follow One Course Until you're Successful.* That's what I did in 1973. I signed up for my first real investment course, and I just did it and did it and did it. I bought this one little $18,000 place, and I did it, again. I did it, again, and I did it, again, until the point where I understood it.

Then I went into becoming an entrepreneur. I did it, and I did it and did it. I'm still learning, and I'm still learning about real estate. It doesn't mean I don't lose. Sometimes I lose. Sometimes I make mistakes. If you're going to be successful as an investor, *diversification is good for the average investor.* If that's what you want to be, have a good life.

What I'd rather do is be able to know the good ones from the bad ones. The good investments from the bad investments. The good advisors from the bad advisors. What's good for me and what's not good for you. That's why I really think. Instead of diversification, the new rules of money say, 'Follow one course until you're successful, and then keep doing it because *once you find the way of being successful, you can do it again and again and again.'*"

Rule #5: Hard Times Bring Opportunities

"The thing is, economies go up, economies go down. We might go into a depression, worldwide. France is in very big trouble. Germany is okay. England is in big trouble. China is in trouble. If we go with that, we go into worldwide depression, and it might take 10 years to come out of it. *During these times is the best time.* I have made more money in the last three years than ever before in my life. I bought five golf courses last year. They're giving them away. But you have to know how to operate them. You have to be an entrepreneur.

This Japanese company had it and they asked me if I wanted to buy it about five years ago, for $260 million. I said, 'It doesn't make sense. It doesn't make sense at $260 million.' They told me I didn't know what I was doing, this and that. 'Okay, bye.' Then, one year ago, Citibank called up and says, 'You want those golf courses?' They gave me the money to buy them."

Rule #6: Design the Business Properly

"In approximately 1975, I came out with this product. We're extremely successful, but we kept running out of money. The more successful we got, the more we ran out of money. That's when I went to my rich dad and I tried to borrow $100,000.

He chewed me out. He says, 'Why would I invest in a dumb product when you have a bad business?' That's when he began to teach me the next level of my entrepreneurial education. *It's not about the product.*

It's about how to design a business that doesn't need me to keep raising capital. In other words, *how do you design a business that keeps raising money automatically?* Today, The Rich Dad Company is cash rich. Cash keeps pouring in because the ability to raise money constantly was designed into the business. Many times, people say, 'I have a great product,' but their legal is really bad. Or their communication systems are bad. Or their internal order processing is bad. Or the manufacturing is bad. Or the marketing is bad. Or they have bad cash flow management."

Rule #7: Know What You're Working For

"There are three types of income. Most people are working hard for *earned income.* The trouble with earned income in America, your tax rate is approximately 50%. Or, as Warren Buffett says, it's a shame that his secretary pays a higher percentage in taxes than he did, although he makes billions.

When you say to a child, 'Go to school and get a safe, secure job,' you're telling them to work for earned income, the worst type of income. The second type of income is *portfolio income,* and today, as I speak, I'm going to try and change this. It's about 20%, and portfolio income is generally known as capital gain. If I buy a stock for $10 and I sell it for $50, the $40 is taxed 20%. Or if I buy a house for $100,000 and I sell it for $200,000, that's a capital gains-type event, so you'd pay a lower tax for that.

The third type of income, which is the best type of income, is *passive income.* This is income that just comes in on a regular basis. One of the reasons I am wealthy and was able to retire at a young age is because I worked hard for passive income, not earned income. I don't flip real estate, generally. Not portfolio income. I don't flip stocks. I want passive income. If you know what you're doing, you can pay 0% taxes legally, and this is done all over the world."

Rule #8: Don't Be Afraid of Losses

"Most successful entrepreneurs have gone bust. Henry Ford, an old-time entrepreneur, he went bust five times. Look at Steve Jobs. His own board fired him. Bill Gates was taken before the Supreme Court for monopolistic practices. Even my friend, Donald Trump, went down a billion dollars. I only went down a million. The average person is so afraid of those losses they never get ahead because at school, they teach you if you make a mistake or if you fail, you're a failure. That's not real life. *A baby learns to walk by standing up and falling down, standing up and falling down.* Our school system punishes you for making mistakes. That's why my poor dad, an academic, was so unsuccessful. He was terrified of making mistakes."

Rule #9: Aim to Acquire Assets

"This is Ken McElroy's company. It's called MC Companies. Ken McElroy's business is in the business of acquiring assets. That's why his company gets richer and richer and richer. Every year he adds, probably, 1,000 new apartment units to his inventory, so Ken's company gets richer and richer because MC Company is designed to increase assets. ***Poorly-designed businesses never have any assets.*** They have huge liabilities. Ken McElroy's business gets stronger and stronger and stronger because, every year, he's increasing in more assets. The Rich Dad Company gets stronger and stronger and stronger because, every year, we add more assets. This year, we're adding franchising to our mix. Also, 'Rich Brother Rich Sister,' the book, has come out. We come out with The Real Book of Real Estate, et cetera, et cetera. Everyone on those products, every year, continues to send money in. That's an idea of a well-designed business. I don't care if it's for real estate or making cash flow board games. If it's well-designed, investors will give money to you because this is a well-designed business."

Rule #10: Stop Saving Money, Hedge It

"I think the big mistake is I hear so many people say, 'It's important to save.' That's ridiculous, and the reason that's ridiculous is because what happened in 1971 is crucial. In 1971, the U.S. dollar stopped being money. In 1971, the U.S. dollar became a currency. The President took us off the gold standard. What's happening is all the savers today are losers. The problem with 1971 is that the federal government keeps printing money, so the value of your money keeps going down. A very big problem for most people is ***stop using the word 'save' and use the word 'hedge.'***

You've got to hedge your money, hedge against losses. When I buy a stock, I put a hedge in. I put a stop-loss or a put inside of it or a call. This has happened throughout history. It happened thousands of years ago, with the Romans, with the Greeks, with the Germans, with the English, the Japanese and the Chinese. Every time they've made money into a currency, something you could print, unlimited. Every time that has happened, the currency has gone to its true value, which is zero."

Robert Kiyosaki Summary

1. Experience Makes You Smarter
2. Give More, Receive More
3. Change the Way You Think
4. Focus
5. Hard Times Bring Opportunities
6. Design the Business Properly
7. Know What You're Working For
8. Don't Be Afraid of Losses
9. Aim to Acquire Assets
10. Stop Saving Money, Hedge It

How can you apply these rules to your business or life today?

_____

_____

_____

_____

_____

_____

_____

_____

_____

_____

#DidYouKnow: Robert Kiyosaki's sister, Emi Kiyosaki, is a former Tibetan Buddhist nun. He co-authored one book with Emy called "Rich Brother, Rich Sister".

"The secret code for everybody is keep your dream alive because it might come through some day." – Jack Ma

- Founder and Executive Chairman of Alibaba
- Started with $20,000 that his wife helped him raise
- 1st mainland Chinese entrepreneur to be on the Forbes cover
- Was 2nd in Fortune's 2017 World's 50 Greatest Leaders list
- 0.3% of annual revenue goes to environmental protection

Rule #1: Get Used to Rejection *[Evan's Fav]*

"For three years I tried, failed in the universities.

So I applied jobs for 30 times, got rejected.

I went for police, they said, 'No, you're not good.'

I even went to KFC.

When KFC came to China, it came to our city.

24 people went for the job.

23 people were accepted.

I was the only guy.

I went for the police.

5 people, 4 of them accepted.

I was the only guy they're not receiving.

I applied for Harvard for 10 times, rejected.

I know I would be rejected.

And then I told myself, *someday I should go teach there.*"

Rule #2: Keep Your Dream Alive

"We have a secret code for success.

Just like 'Open sesame' is the secret code for Alibaba, the secret code for everybody is *keep your dream alive because it might come through some day.*

This is what the secret code is."

Rule #3: Have A Good Name

Interviewer: "Why did you call it Alibaba?"

Jack Ma: "Alibaba?

Well, when I started, I thought, the Internet is global. We should have a global name, and a name that is interesting.

At that time, the best name was Yahoo!

So I've been thinking for many days. Suddenly I thought Alibaba is a good name. I happened to be in San Francisco that day, having lunch, and a waitress comes.

I asked her, 'Do you know about Alibaba?' She said, 'Yes.' I say, 'What is Alibaba?' She said, *'Open sesame.' Good!*

So I went on the street, asked about 10, 20 people. They all know about Alibaba, the 40 thieves and open sesame, and I think this a good name. And it starts with A.

Whatever you talk about, Alibaba's always top."

Rule #4: Build Trust

"When we started in e-commerce nobody believed that China would have e-commerce because people believed in face-to-face and all kind of networks in the traditional way.

There's no trust system in China. Every day we finish more than 30 million transactions. And that means that there, you are buying things from somebody you have never seen.

You are giving products to the person you have never met. And some guy you have never met is going to take your products to that place, to that person.

I want to tell the people that the trust is there. *It's all about the trust.*"

Rule #5: Get Inspired

"I learned a lot of things from movies.

I learned how to make a speech from the movie called 'The Bodyguard' with Whitney Houston. When she sings the songs, I look at her, 'Wow!'

That's the way that you make a speech.

Because I never knew how to make speech. Because I'm not an actor. But when I saw the movie, I said, 'Wow!'

If you sing from your heart, if you sing naturally, if you are yourself, so I realized. And I learned a lot from the movies.

I even learned from The Godfathers. *My favorite movie is Forrest Gump.* These are the things I learned so much from.

Then I would discuss about the muse, the inspirations we got from movies."

Rule #6: Stay Focused

Interviewer: "What kinds of business ideas have you said no to?"

Jack Ma: "I'm saying 'No' to a lot of ideas because as a CEO, I have to say 'No' to opportunities, because if I say 'Yes,' I probably get 5,000 opportunities everyday.

But whether yes or no, *everything is based on the mission, helping doing business easier.*

If it's on that, we'll consider.

If somebody comes and says, 'We'll make a lot of money,'

I'm not interested."

Rule #7: Focus On Culture

"Culture.

It's not the technology.

I think **technology is a tool.**

The core competence of our company is we have grown from 18 people to now, 20,000 young people.

And we focus a lot on the value, the mission and making sure the culture, **everybody works for helping others, instead of just making money."**

Rule #8: Customers Are #1

"We believe the core company is different from Wall Street.

We believe customer, number one, employee, number two, shareholder, number three.

Customer one, employee two, shareholder three.

Shareholder, number three.

This is my religion.

It's the customer that pays us the money.

It's the employees that drive the innovation.

I remember the day before the IPO, and a lot of people said, 'Jack, give us the shares, we were long term shareholders.'

But when the crisis came, these guys ran.

My people stayed. Customers stayed."

Rule #9: Don't Complain, Look for Opportunities

"I want to tell young people: Most people complain, 'Where's the opportunity?' People started complaining. Some people complain, some people start to change themselves, changing others. *Where the opportunity is, is where the complaints are.* Where's the trouble, where's the opportunity. And I always believed that."

Rule #10: Have Passion

"Today, we are all here to discuss what we should do in the *next five to 10 years*. So what will Alibaba become in the future? I've always said our competitors are not domestic websites but overseas websites. Our competitors are not in China but in Silicon Valley.

So first, we should position Alibaba as a global website not just a domestic website. Second, we need to learn the *hardworking spirit* of Silicon Valley. If we go to work at 8 a.m. and go home at 5 p.m., this is not a high-tech company and Alibaba will never be successful. If we have that kind of 8-5 spirit, then we should just go and do something else.

Americans are strong at hardware and systems. But on information and software, Chinese brains are *just as good* as theirs. All of our brains are just as good as theirs. This is the reason we dare to compete with Americans. If we are a good team and know what we want to do, one of us can defeat tons of them.

We can beat government agencies and big famous companies because of our *innovative spirit*. Otherwise what is the difference between us and them? Everyone knows the Internet is a bubble. It keeps getting bigger and bigger, but when will it burst? Yahoo!'s stock will fall, and eBay's stock will rise. And maybe after eBay's stock rises, Alibaba's stock will rise. So don't worry. The dream of the Internet won't burst. We will have to pay a painful price in the next three to five years. *It is the only way we can succeed.*"

Jack Ma Summary

1. Get Used to Rejection
2. Keep Your Dream Alive
3. Have a Good Name
4. Build Trust
5. Get Inspired
6. Stay Focused
7. Focus on Culture
8. Customers Are #1
9. Don't Complain, Look for Opportunities
10. Have Passion

How can you apply these rules to your business or life today?

_____

_____

_____

_____

_____

_____

_____

_____

_____

_____

_____

#DidYouKnow: In 2007, in response to worldwide criticism of the practice of killing sharks for their fins, Ma announced that he and his family had 'sworn off shark fin soup now and forever.'

"Everybody wants to fulfill the highest truest expression of yourself as a human being." – Oprah Winfrey

- Media icon, actress, producer, and philanthropist
- The Oprah Winfrey Show was the top rated show of its kind
- Often considered the most influential woman in the world
- Born into poverty in Mississippi to a teenage single mom
- Is the greatest black philanthropist in American history

Rule #1: Understand the Next Move

"The way through the challenge is to get still and ask yourself, *'What is the next right move?'*

Not think about, 'Oh I got all of this to do.'

What is the next right move?

And then from that space, make the next right move and the next right move.

And not to be overwhelmed by it because you know your life is bigger than that one moment.

You know you're not defined by what somebody says is a failure for you because *failure is just there to point you in a different direction."*

Rule #2: Seize Your Opportunity

"Nothing about my life is lucky. Nothing.

A lot of grace, a lot of blessings, a lot of divine order, but I don't believe in luck.

For me *luck is preparation meeting the moment of opportunity.*

There is no luck without you being prepared to handle that moment of opportunity.

What I would say for myself is that because of my hand and a force greater than my own, I had been prepared in ways that I didn't even know I was being prepared for.

And the truth is, for me and *for every person, every single thing that has ever happened in your life is preparing you for the moment that is to come."*

Rule #3: Have No Embarrassment

"You know, *there's no such thing to me as an embarrassing moment*. No such thing.

If I tripped and fell, if my bra strap showed, if my slip fell off, if I fell flat on my face, there's no such thing as an embarrassing moment.

Because I know that *there's not a moment that I could possibly experience on the air that somebody hasn't already experienced.*

So when it happens, you say, 'Oh, my slip fell off!' And it's no big deal."

Rule #4: Work On Yourself

"I say to my girls all of the time that your real work is to figure out where your power base is and to work on the *alignment of your personality, your gifts that you have to give, with the real reason why you're here.*

That's the number one thing you have to do.

Work on yourself and fill yourself up and keep your cup full.

Keep yourself full.

Now I used to be afraid of that, I used to be afraid. Particularly from people who say, 'Oh she's so full of herself, she's so full.'

And now I embrace it. I consider it a compliment that I am full of myself because only when you're full, I'm full, I'm overflowing, my cup runneth over, I have so much to offer and *so much to give* and I am not afraid of honoring myself.

It's miraculous when you think about it."

Rule #5: Run as Hard as You Can

"Every season somebody else was coming out. One talk show, two talk shows, three talk shows. There'd been over a 100 talk shows since we started, but every time, I would feel like, "Alright, got to step up our game. Got to step up our game.' The way you step up your game is not to worry about the other guy in any situation because you can't control the other guy. *You only have control over yourself.*

So it's like running a race. The energy that it takes to look back and see where the other guys are takes energy away from you and if they're too close it scares you. So that's what I would say to my team all the time. *Don't waste your time in the race looking back* to see where the other guy is or what the other guy is doing. It's not about the other guy, it's about what can you do? You just need to run that race as hard as you can. You need to give it everything you've got all the time for yourself."

Rule #6: #Believe *[Evan's Fav]*

"My grandmother was a maid. That's all she ever knew. The only real expectation she held for me was that I would one day become a maid and in her words, 'Have some good white folks,' meaning people who would not speak negatively about me, who would allow me to take food home, who would be good to me. That was my grandmother's dream for me. But I had another dream for myself. More than a dream, *I had a belief for myself.* I remember watching her hang out clothes on a line one day and say to me, 'You have to watch me Oprah Gail because one day you'll have to do this for yourself,' and knowing inside myself that that was not going to be my life. I don't know how I knew it other than that thing that we all have, intuition or instinct, that said 'No, this will not be my life.' I knew that I would not be hanging clothes on a line in a backyard in Mississippi.

So I was either four or five years old and that belief that that would not be my life is what I held onto for the longest of times. I just, no matter what, *believed that there was something bigger, greater, more for me.*"

Rule #7: We're Seeking the Same Thing

"I always understood that there really was no difference between me and the audience. At times, I might have had better shoes, but at the core of what really matters, that we are the same.

And you know how I know that?

Because all of us are *seeking the same thing.* You will go out into the world and each pursue, based upon what you believe your talents are, what your skills are, maybe your gifts are.

But you're seeking the same thing. *Everybody wants to fulfill the highest truest expression of yourself as a human being.* That's what you're looking for, the highest truest expression of yourself as a human being.

And because I understand that, I understand that if you're working in a bakery, and that's where you want to be, and that may be what you always wanted to do, is to bake pies for people or bake cakes for people or *to offer your gift,* then that's for you and there's no difference between you and me except that's your platform.

That's your show every day.

So my understanding of that has allowed me to reach everyone and there's no way that you wouldn't because that's what I truly feel."

Rule #8: Find Your Purpose

"A lot of people don't know their purpose and if you don't know your purpose, your immediate goal is to *figure that out* because otherwise you're just wandering around here.

So the moment you can figure out what it is *you're supposed to be doing,* the sooner you're able to get about the business of doing that."

Rule #9: Stay Grounded

"My life is fueled by my being, and the being fuels the doing, so I come from a **centered place**. I come from a **focused place.**

I come from **compassion,** it's just my nature. I come from a **willingness to understand** and to be understood and I come from **wanting to connect.**

The secret of that show for 25 years is that people could see themselves in me all over the world. They could see themselves in me.

And even as I became more and more financially successful, which was a big surprise to me, it was like, 'Oh my God, this is so exciting.'

What I realized is through the whole process, because I'm **grounded in my own self,** that although I could have more shoes, my feet stayed on the ground, although I was wearing better shoes.

I could understand that it really was because I was grounded.

I was doing, and continue to this day, to do the consciousness work. I work at staying awake."

Rule #10: Relax, It's Going to Be Okay

"Dear beautiful brown-skinned girl. And I use the word 'beautiful' because I know that's never a word you would call yourself.

I look into your eyes and I see the light and hope of myself. In this photo, you're just about to turn 20, posing outside the television station where you were recently hired as a reporter.

You look calm, you look happy, but I know how scared you are. If I could say anything to you it would be, **'Relax, it's going to be okay girl.'"**

Oprah Winfrey Summary

1. Understand the Next Move
2. Seize Your Opportunity
3. Have No Embarrassment
4. Work On Yourself
5. Run as Hard as You Can
6. #Believe
7. We're Seeking the Same Thing
8. Find Your Purpose
9. Stay Grounded
10. Relax, It's Going to Be Okay

How can you apply these rules to your business or life today?

_____

_____

_____

_____

_____

_____

_____

_____

_____

_____

_____

#DidYouKnow: Oprah Winfrey's original birth name is 'Orpah' and her company name, Harpo, is Oprah spelled backwards.

"We have two primary choices in life: Accept conditions as they exist or take the responsibility to change them." – Les Brown

- Motivational speaker, author, and former politician
- Known for his catch phrase "It's Possible!"
- Selected as one of America's top 5 speakers by Toastmasters
- Born in an abandoned building in a low-income part of Miami
- Received an Emmy for his 'You Deserve with Les Brown'

Rule #1: #Believe in Yourself

"I do a lot of training for many corporations and I conduct sales seminars. I've heard all kind of guys doing techniques and training people. Techniques of how to close sales and how to work within and begin to control the sale and how to ask for the close. Let me share something with you. You can learn all the techniques in the world. *If you don't believe in yourself, it won't happen for you.* I learned all of it. That's why I do a training called 'Focus on the Seller.'

You've got to focus on you and as you convince you, as you sell yourself every day, every day, every day, you will begin to see a difference in the things that you're doing. Selling yourself on your ability to perform a job, to achieve a certain objective, telling yourself every day, 'Here I go again and I got what it takes. *This is my day and nothing out here is going to stop me.*'"

Rule #2: Amaze Your Customers

"It's necessary that you *be flexible.* That you are always thinking, 'How can I improve this?' This is a customer-driven economy. It's necessary for you to always explore various ways in which you can improve the quality of service that you're providing for the people in your organization.

I remember something a major company had talked about, the extra value service they were providing for their customers. And the lady who had the news conference summarized it this way. She said 'It's not our intention to satisfy our customers or to please our customers. *Our intention is to amaze them.*' It's necessary if you're going to compete today that you look for ways to amaze your customers by being one of those individuals that keep your commitments, that keep your word, that's relentless.

It's necessary as you work with the people that you bring into your organization that they see that you are a good example of a person to work with because you model *integrity,* and *determination,* and *ambition,* and *truth,* and *honesty* in the way in which you conduct business."

Rule #3: Take Responsibility *[Evan's Fav]*

"Take full responsibility for your life. Accept where you are and the responsibility that you're going to take yourself where you want to go. *We have two primary choices in life: We can either accept conditions as they exist, or we can take the responsibility to change them.* People want to exempt themselves from taking responsibility. All they want to do is talk about the problem. Every time you see them, they'll tell you their story over and over and over and over again. No. No! You want to take responsibility for your life. 'I got me here. I can get me out of this. And I'm getting out. I'm not going to be a volunteer victim.' So part of beginning to get unstuck, you've got to decide that the behavior pattern that you have adopted doesn't work for you. You've got to change your strategies and changing your strategy means reinventing your life. Recreating you and you have the power to do that. You can decide that you're going to change, that you're not going to be a wimp. You can decide that you're going to stand up to life. You can decide that I'm going to live each day as if it were my last. You have the power to make that decision. You can decide, I'm going to work on myself and develop myself. *I'm going to empower me.* And all of these things that are happening to me right now, they're just temporary inconveniences. They're not stronger than I am. I'm in charge here."

Rule #4: Stand Up to Yourself

"Overcoming the negative conversation, that inner dialogue that's going on all the time, even when you don't want it to be there. You've got to stand up inside yourself sometimes and say, *'Shut up! You've got to do this.'* I was going to give a presentation, and this voice inside of me saying, 'You can't do this. You don't have everything it takes.' I said, 'Shut up! I'm behind on my bills and you're telling me what I can't do. I have got to do it!' You get scared sometimes. Your mind will go blank on you. Some people you will allow to unnerve you. And you wonder, 'What's wrong with me?' That's why you've got to learn to make a conscious, deliberate, determined effort to stand up inside yourself. Working on yourself, watching that inner dialogue, it will determine the quality of your life."

Rule #5: Go All Out

"You've got to activate the thinker in you. ***Don't allow your emotions to control you.*** If you don't discipline and contain your emotions, they will use you. Your mind goes on automatic, just like a garden. Weeds don't have to have any encouragement to grow. You don't have to water them. They don't have to get sunshine. They don't have to have fertile ground. They will grow through the cracks of a sidewalk. But if you want to grow orchids or roses or any kind of exotic flowers, there are special processes and procedures you must go through. You don't have to force yourself or motivate yourself to think negatively, to be depressed, to hate somebody, to want revenge, to want to get back at somebody, to beat yourself up over the head, to feel loaded with guilt. You don't have to make any effort to do that. You've got to be willing to harness your will. Your mind is on automatic. It will do that by itself. But if you want to begin to move into your own personal greatness, if you want to begin to really enjoy a happy successful healthy life, you've got to be willing to go against the tide. You've got to be willing to harness your will and say, 'In spite of this, I'm in control here. I'm not going to let this get me down. I'm not going to let this destroy me. I'm coming back and I'll be stronger and better because of it.' You have got to make a declaration that this is what you stand for. ***You're standing up for your dreams.*** You're standing up for peace of mind. You're standing up for health. You want it and you're going to go all out to have it. It's not going to be easy. When you want a change, it's not easy. If it were in fact easy, everybody would do it. But if you're serious, you'll go all out."

Rule #6: Stay Busy

"I don't care how good you are, I don't care how talented you are, I don't care how much you work on yourself, there's some times when things aren't going to go right. They just are not going to go right. Why? I don't know why. That's called life. And you have to deal with it. Sometimes your life will be in a slump. Just like sports. Some of the best shooters can't hit baskets. They get in a slump. Do they sit on the sideline? No. They continue to execute. ***If you are facing a challenge, don't stop. Stay busy. Work your plan. Continue to move. Stay busy, stay busy, stay busy.***"

Rule #7: Give More Than You're Paid For

"I was working on a job and I came home one day and I told my former wife, 'That guy Burt I work for is stupid.' That night I could not sleep well. Here was a guy that was controlling my life. The truth that I had to come to grips with that I wasn't in charge of my destiny. The truth was that I wasn't giving all that I had. The truth was that there are some things that I wanted to do but I didn't have the courage to act on those things. And the truth was that Burt Childs was a blessing to me. He made life so miserable for me, I had to start looking at my life differently.

I started going to work earlier. I started being the last one to leave there. I started working harder than anybody else. The other guys: 'Why would you work so hard, Les?' I said, 'I'm not working for them.' I had been cheating Burt, I thought. I'd been cheating myself and my family. Wherever you are, whatever you're doing, do it with everything that you have. Develop the habit of giving more than what you're paid for. ***Develop the habit of setting standards that others will be measured by.*** Do not go where the path may lead, but go where there's no path and leave a trail."

Rule #8: Someone's Opinion Is Not Reality

"In the process of working on your dreams, you are going to incur a lot of disappointment, a lot of failure, a lot of pain, a lot of setbacks, a lot of defeats. But in the process of doing that, you will discover some things about yourself that you don't know right now. What you will realize is that **you have greatness within you.** What you will realize is that you are more powerful than you can ever begin to imagine. What you will realize is that you are greater than your circumstances, that you don't have to go through life being a victim. I met a high school teacher who one day changed my life. I was waiting on another student and when he came in he said to me, 'Young man, go to the board and write what I'm about to tell you.' And I said, 'I can't do that, sir.' And he said, 'Why not?' I said, 'Because I'm educable mentally retarded.' And he came from behind his desk and he looked at me. He said, 'Don't ever say that again. ***Someone's opinion of you does not have to become your reality.***'"

Rule #9: You're Different

"Inoculate yourself with positive words to make yourself unstoppable. Get out of your mind the polluting negative thoughts that's causing most people to go through life being stuck because they're volunteer victims. Many people die at age 25 and don't get buried until they're 65 because they got so much garbage in their minds. You're here because you got a clear vision of what you want and where you're going. **You want more. You're different than everybody else.** Don't worry if they don't get it. Don't try and convince people. A person convinced against their will is of the same opinion still. You are not like everybody else. You can walk outside and find pigeons but if you're looking for eagles, it's going to take you a minute. You are different. It's lonely at the top. It's lonely at the top but you eat better."

Rule #10: Don't Stop

"It's hard changing your life. It was hard when just over three years ago in the Penobscot Building in Detroit, Michigan, where I was operating my business, and I fell on some hard times and I was sleeping in my office. It was hard coming into the lobby and the security said, 'Excuse me, Mr. Brown, can we see you for a moment?' And I said, 'Yes.' And I walked up to the counter and he gave me an envelope. I opened the envelope and the envelope was from management that said, 'This is an office tower, it's not a hotel. Please do not sleep in your office.' And I said, 'Excuse me, sir, I just work long hours in creating my business. I'm an entrepreneur and right now things are bad for me, but they're not going to be this way always. And I just ask for the opportunity to continue to operate like I'm doing. I'm not trying to make this my home.' And it was hard coming through the lobby, and sometimes they would laugh, 'There's the guy talking about becoming successful and look at him. He's bathing in the bathroom upstairs on the 21st floor. He sleeps on the floor. Look at him.' It was hard, ladies and gentlemen. Coming to speak to people and I was facing financial difficulties in my own life. Don't stop. Don't stop. Don't stop running toward your dream. For those of you that have experienced some hardships, **don't give up on your dream.** Don't stop running toward your dream."

Les Brown Summary

1. #Believe in Yourself
2. Amaze Your Customers
3. Take Responsibility
4. Stand Up to Yourself
5. Go All Out
6. Stay Busy
7. Give More Than You're Paid For
8. Someone's Opinion is Not Reality
9. You're Different
10. Don't Stop

How can you apply these rules to your business or life today?

_____

_____

_____

_____

_____

_____

_____

_____

_____

_____

_____

_____

_____

#DidYouKnow: Les Brown ran for election in the Ohio House of Representatives and won.

"I'm a humungous believer that ideas are sh** and that execution is the game." – Gary Vaynerchuk

- Entrepreneur, investor, author, and VaynerMedia founder
- VaynerMedia does social media services for the Fortune 500
- Grew his father's liquor store from $3 million to $50 million
- Described as "the first wine guru of the YouTube era"
- Best known as a digital marketing and social-media pioneer

Rule #1: Bet On Your Strengths

"You need to bet on your strengths, and don't give f*** about what you suck at.

Way too many people are going to spend the next 30, 40 years of their lives, trying to check the boxes of the things that they're not as good at, and you're going to waste a load of time, and lose.

I highly recommend auditing yourself, or if you have no empathy, or E.Q., or self-awareness, then find somebody in your family or friendship that does, and let them tell you who you are, and once you believe that, either for yourself or someone else told you, go directly all chips, all in to that, because that is the only possible way.

That is a very highly likely way of overindexing, because the truth is, *if you want to be an anomaly, you've got to act like one."*

Rule #2: Work

"How do you get money to do what you love? You don't.

I lost a load of money when I started doing what I loved.

What you do, is you *position yourself to succeed.*

So, for example, if you're doing something else, and you want to do this thing you love, you do it after hours.

You work nine to six, you get home, you kiss the dog, and you go to town.

You start building equity in your brand and whatever you're trying to accomplish after hours.

Everybody has time.

Stop watching 'Lost.' If you want this, if you want bling bling, if you want to buy the Jets, work. That's how you get it."

Rule #3: Put Business in Perspective

"The way I handle things, even on the few rare days when I really struggle, I take a real step back, and make pretend that somebody called me and told me that my mother or daughter were killed. And I know that's very dark, and I apologize, but it's really what I do.

I literally am able to, at my deepest most struggling moment within business, take a step back and remind myself that I could make a drillion dollars tomorrow on Bitcoin and if something bad happened to the people I love the most, then it would mean nothing, and it *very consistently rewires me very quickly.*

I just put *business in perspective.* At the end of the day, for me it's not really money, it's my legacy. I put it in perspective.

And you know what? Up until I had a daughter, even while I was married, up until when I had Misha, four years ago, I secretly wanted to lose all my money. I had this weird twisted dark fantasy of losing everything just to rise again like a phoenix and remind you."

Rule #4: Execute Your Ideas

"I'm a humungous believer in that ideas are sh** and that execution's the game. We've all got ideas. Everybody's got ideas. Do you know how many f***ing ideas we all have here? We can probably sit here for the next two hours, draw them all out, record them, and predict the next 78 great startups over the next nine years.

There is way too much fodder brought to the idea. Uber was Magic Cab, three years earlier. Uber's not an idea, Uber existed. It was called Magic Cab.

But the guys that executed it sucked, so they lost. If there's any level of romance left in this room about your idea, I'd like to suffocate it, because I think *the actual situation is what you actually do with it."*

Rule #5: Don't Overlook Storytelling

"Storytelling is the most under-rated skill in business because I don't think people realize it's happening when it's happening, and most of all, I don't think that many people are really good at it. When I watch a Steve Jobs keynote about a new product, I don't care about the new tech, I don't care about the iPad or the iPhone, *I care about the way he was presenting it.* When I see David Blaine, this is a magician, if you ever pay attention to what he's doing, he's storytelling you the whole way, and then it's the big kick. So if you understand what the consumer wants, then you backtrack and you tell the story to get them emotionally there, that's how things sell. That's marketing. The reason I think that people are missing why things succeed is because of storytelling. I think it's overlooked. I think that people look at the x's and o's and the black and the white, but I think storytelling, when done right, takes a product that should have sold a hundred million dollars' worth of stuff, and sells a billion dollars' worth."

Rule #6: Care About Your Customers

"In 2001, it snowed on December 23rd, the busiest day of the year in the liquor store. A woman called us and her case of Beringer White Zinfandel wasn't delivered. The entire case cost $45. We're doing about $40,000 an hour in the store. She calls. I find out about it. I was on the floor selling. I am the premier salesman on the floor and we're debating what to do. She needs it for her Christmas dinner. I grab the case, throw it in my car, and drive to deliver it. It takes me 2 1/2 hours. The woman was 194 years old. We didn't have a lot of lifetime value on the back end there. She looked like Yoda. And the best part was, I delivered it, all pumped with myself, and she said, 'great,' and closed the door. Awesome. Everybody, especially my Dad, was pissed that I left, because of all the customers that came in asking for me, or that I could have sold, everybody's baffled. I can't tell you what the ROI of driving through the snow in my car to deliver a case of $45 pink sh** to a woman that looked like Yoda was. But I can tell you this. Over the next three years, *that story became the foundation of how we treated every single customer.* It became our competitive edge, and those are the things that matter to me."

Rule #7: Stick to Your DNA

"The ability to adjust is the entire game.

I'm so proud that I change my mind every day.

My ability to only be comfortable in massive chaos has been my biggest asset as an entrepreneur.

You need to do you. It's so damn important to stick to your DNA.

Recognize that you need to surround yourself, whether it's your co-founder, or whether it's the people who work for you.

All I do is hire the people that are the opposite of me, that bring the other value, that bring me the ability to remember what that meeting was about and go make sure it happens."

Rule #8: Do the Things That Matter

"I delegate everything that I think is not the single most important thing in the world and then I micromanage the things that I think are the most important things in the world.

Luckily, I don't think most things matter.

I don't think I'm any different than anybody else. I actually think everybody is a delegator and a micromanager.

I just think that my radar of what's important is different.

The difference is, *I don't think most things matter.*

Like one client that's going to put us out of business. I don't think one employee is going to kill our atmosphere. I don't think a lot of things matter.

I don't think a misspelling in a deck is something that really matters."

Rule #9: Don't Make Excuses *[Evan's Fav]*

"I think the **biggest obstacle to success is a lack of optimism.** There will always be problems. Let's talk about a million other things that are a way to stop success. The health and well-being of your family members, so it takes your mind away from execution. The country you live in's government and political concepts at these moments. There's a competitor with a billion dollars who's also skilled and punches you in the mouth and knocks you out in the first round. There's just a million obstacles. **You've just got to persevere.** These are moments in time. There are a million reasons why not, but there's one great reason why. It's hard being an entrepreneur. It's hard building a business. Everybody thinks it's so easy, that there's an entitlement. Building a business is hard, and you know what makes it really hard? Everything that happens every day of every moment, so, you can pick time, you can pick money, as the one or two things that you think stop you from winning your game, but the truth is, there's a million reasons.

I will never make an excuse, everything that's a problem with me, everything I don't achieve, everything that's a problem with VaynerMedia, and everything is my fault, and I succumb to that and I respect that, and I actually think that's the way it should be. And so no excuses, my friends."

Rule #10: There Is No Overnight Success

"Nothing in life is free. Nothing happens overnight. It all takes tons and tons of work and tons and tons of **talent, and tons and tons of serendipity,** but my friends, luck, serendipity, there's a forced culture within that. You don't just sit in your room hoping and then something lucky happens. Nobody just knocks on your house's door and says, 'Congratulations, you've been awarded this.' **Luck comes from being in the right spot.** I've been really lucky, because I bleed out of my eyes every day of my life and worked my face off. There's no overnight successes, period. They don't exist. Show me. Leave a comment in YouTube. Leave the name. Explain to me. Tell me. Show me. Let me know. Show me the overnight success, because I'll show you you, justifying in your brain, something that is just not true. Period."

Gary Vaynerchuk Summary

1. Bet On Your Strengths
2. Work
3. Put Business in Perspective
4. Execute Your Ideas
5. Don't Overlook Storytelling
6. Care About Your Customers
7. Stick to Your DNA
8. Do the Things That Matter
9. Don't Make Excuses
10. There Is No Overnight Success

How can you apply these rules to your business or life today?

_____

_____

_____

_____

_____

_____

_____

_____

_____

_____

#DidYouKnow: Gary Vaynerchuk immigrated to America from Belarus in 1978 and lived with eight family members in a studio apartment.

"There are no accidents. We all show up here with a purpose. Don't die with your music still in you." – Wayne Dyer

- Self-help author and motivational speaker
- Your Erroneous Zones was his first book
- It's one of the best-selling books of all time
- The book success led to more books and lecture tours
- Lists Saint Francis of Assisi and Lao Tzu among his influences

Rule #1: You Can't Give Away What You Don't Have

"You can't give away what you don't have. Now it sounds ridiculous. But it's more than what meets the ear as you hear this. You can't give away what you don't have. People who are not good at giving away love can't give away love because they don't have it to give away.

If I want to give you a dozen oranges, I can't give you those dozen oranges unless I go out and pick up 12 oranges someplace. Otherwise all it is just empty rhetoric. And the same thing is true of virtually everything in your life.

You can't give away love for others if you don't have love in here to give away.

If what you have in here is contempt. If what you have in here is anger. If what you have in here is fear, then these are the things you're going to be giving away in your life."

Rule #2: Don't Identify Yourself With What You Accomplish

"The second thing that the ego teaches us is that who I am is not only what I have, but who I am is *what I do, what I accomplish.*

And so we spend a big chunk of our lives, believing that the way that we become *'successful,' 'happy,' 'fulfilled,' 'self-extoled,'* whatever it might be, is on the basis of what I accomplish, what my resume looks like, how many promotions I get. And so we send our children off to school and we ask them to learn, to identify themselves on how much they get and what they accomplish.

Your grades become more important than what it is that you are studying. What you own, what clothes you wear, what labels you have, and so on, and we become *obsessed with this kind of absurdity, and this is the false self at work.*"

Rule #3: As You Think, So Shall You Be

"There are many ways to get the things that we want for ourselves in our lives, but basically it all begins with how we choose to think. As you think, so shall you be. Seven little words that I think are perhaps the most important things that we can learn and master in our lives. This old proverb notion that *I become what I think about all day long,* and once you know that what you think about is what expands, you start getting real careful about what you think about. You don't allow your thoughts to be on anything that you don't want, or that you wouldn't want to have manifest or show up for you in your life."

Rule #4: Be Open-Minded

"Have a mind that is open to everything and attached to nothing. No one knows enough to be a pessimist about anything, and each of us, when we close our mind to what is possible for us, or what is possible for humanity, closes off the genius that resides and lives in each and every one of us. Having an open mind doesn't necessarily mean finding fault with all of the things that you have been taught by others. It means **opening yourself up to the potentiality and the possibility that anything and everything is possible.** So having a mind that is open to everything and attached to nothing really means finding within ourselves the ability to get rid of a trait that I find so common in the contemporary world. Do you know that most people that I meet spend their lives looking for occasions to be offended? They actually are out there hoping that they can find some reason to be offended. And there's no shortage of reasons. They're out there, everywhere. The way this person dressed. What this person said. They turned on their TV. They hear the news. They're offended by this. Someone used language that they didn't like. Someone doesn't share the same customs that you. And people all day long in fact, if you keep track tomorrow, you will find probably a hundred reasons that you can go around being offended. But a mind that is open to everything and attached to nothing is a mind that says, **'I'm never looking for anything to be offended by.'** And that whatever anybody else out there has to say, my response to that is, 'That's an interesting point of view. I've never considered that before.'"

Rule #5: Change How You Look at Things

"When you change the way you look at things, the things you look at change. Albert Einstein once observed that you have the most fundamental and major decision that you have to make in your life is this:

Do I live in a friendly or a hostile universe? Which is it? Is it a universe that is filled with hostility and anger and people wanting to hate each other, and people wanting to kill each other. Is that what you see?

Because when you see the world that way, that's exactly what you will create for yourself in your life. This is from great scientific minds, and the interesting thing is that this is not just a clever play on words. *When you change the way you look at things, the things you look at change.* It's actually a very scientific thing.

You're the one with the struggle, the difficulties, and expecting somebody else to change, or something outside of you to get better, in order for you to make your life work at this level that I'm calling intention, is something you have to really take a hard look at."

Rule #6: Don't Put Boundaries on You

"I used to say that before I had children, I had eight theories about how to raise children. And now I have eight children, and no theories. But one of the things I know about children, is that *no one likes being told what to do.* And this isn't just children, this is all of us.

Don't put boundaries on me. Don't tell me what I can do and what I can't do. Don't tell me how to be there. Don't tell me what to wear, what to think. Don't tell me even how to do yoga. Don't tell me. I don't want to be told. This is the soul speaking, always.

The soul is *constantly having a desire to expand and grow,* and anything or anyone that comes into your life that attempts to do that, you will find yourself fighting it and reaching back."

Rule #7: There Are No Justified Resentments

"There are no justified resentments. This is a difficult principle to get but one that I believe very strongly in. If you carry around resentment inside of you, and I'm talking about the person that you lent money to and hasn't paid you back, the person in your life that you feel was abusive in your life, the person who walked out on you and left you for somebody else, all of the things that you have justified in your heart and in your life that you have the right to be resentful about. *Those resentments will always end up harming you and creating in you a sense of despair.* No one ever dies from a snake bite. It's the venom that continues to pour through your system after the bite that will end up destroying you."

Rule #8: Stop Finding Excuses

"As I think about this idea of getting what you really want, and being able to attract it into your life, what we have to look at is basically the *obstacles that we have conditioned ourselves.* I have never believed that we need to be putting the responsibility on someone else. If you're conditioned it's because you have allowed yourself to become that. We conditioned ourselves to believe certain kinds of things and one of the things that we believe and hang on to, and live with is this whole idea that all of the things that happened to me in my past are what are keeping me from doing what I'd like to do today. *So we hang on to these things and we fill ourselves with blame.* You say, 'I'm the middle child. I'm the youngest child. I'm the oldest child. I'm an only child.' If you're the youngest child you can say, 'Well how could I be making decisions for myself when I always had somebody else telling me what to do my whole life?' If you're the oldest, 'Well, how could I be expected to think for myself, I always had to think for somebody else.' And that leaves the middle child, the classic identity crisis, 'Oh poor me.' So everybody, with their birth order, or with their mother liked their sister better, or that we had enough, or we didn't have enough, or we had too much, or we lived in the North, we lived in the South, I'm too tall, I'm too short, I've got too much hair, I don't have enough hair. Now there goes your life in this direction."

Rule #9: Walk Down Another Street

"Portia Nelson was asked to write the autobiography of her life in five chapters. She wrote: 'One. I walk down the street. There's a deep hole in the sidewalk. I fall in. I'm lost. I'm helpless. It isn't my fault and it takes forever to find a way out. Two. I walk down the same street. There's a deep hole in the sidewalk. I pretend I don't see it. I fall in again. I can't believe I'm in the same place. It isn't my fault. It still takes a long time for me to get out. Three. I walk down the same street. There's a deep hole in the sidewalk. I see it there. I still fall in, it's a habit, but my eyes are open. I know where I am and it is my own fault and I get out immediately. Four. I walk down the same street. There's a deep hole in the sidewalk. I walk around it. *Five. Finally, I walk down another street.*'"

Rule #10: Don't Die With Your Music Still In You *[Evan's Fav]*

"*Some of us hear a different drummer. We must march to the music that we hear.* All of you have some music playing and all of you have a heroic mission. There's no accidents in this universe. We all show up here with a purpose. There's an intelligence that is a part of everything and everyone and all of us are connected to it. Too many of us are afraid to listen to that music and march to it. You out there, I know you have a book you wanted to write. I know there's a composition you wanted to compose. I know there's a song you want to sing. Maybe you want to raise horses out in Montana. Maybe you just want to travel and see the world. Maybe you want to go into a relationship with someone but you've been afraid but your heart says it's the right thing to do. I've known what my music is. It's playing right now, as I stand here in front of you and as I sit down and write my books and tell the world what I know are my truths. I feel always completely on-purpose and fulfilled. And no time will I ever come to the end of my life and say, 'What if my whole life has been wrong?' Whoever you are, whatever that music is, however distant it may sound, however strange, however weird others may interpret it to be, don't get to the end of your life and know that you're going to leave and not have it played yet. *Don't die with your music still in you.*"

Wayne Dyer Summary

1. You Can't Give Away What You Don't Have
2. Don't Identify Yourself With What You Accomplish
3. As You Think, So Shall You Be
4. Be Open-Minded
5. Change How You Look at Things
6. Don't Put Boundaries on You
7. There Are No Justified Resentments
8. Stop Finding Excuses
9. Walk Down Another Street
10. Don't Die With Your Music Still In You

How can you apply these rules to your business or life today?

_____

_____

_____

_____

_____

_____

_____

_____

_____

_____

_____

#DidYouKnow: Wayne Dyer's book, Your Erroneous Zones, has sold over 35 million copies to date.

"Living in service. I feel that is the purest form of joy. Your life means something to somebody other than you." – Will Smith

- Actor, producer, rapper, and songwriter
- Named 'the most powerful actor in Hollywood' by Newsweek
- Starred in NBC television series The Fresh Prince of Bel-Air
- Only actor with 8 consecutive films grossing > $100 million
- Has a Guinness record for attending 3 premieres 24 hours

Rule #1: Improve Yourself

"The concept of improving lives runs through the center of everything I do.

And then I realized that the way to improve lives is to continually *improve yourself.*

So with that, every morning when I get out of the bed, I haven't fixed everything in the world yet.

So there's always something to do.

I read an interesting quote from Buddha.

He said that *good people have to get out of the bed every day and try to empty the ocean with a ladle.*

I knew that was profound. I paused for a second and I said, 'All right, what the hell is a ladle? Okay. It's like a soup spoon.'

So trying to empty the ocean with a soup spoon as the mentality of *how you wake up every day to try to do good in the world.*

I'm really driven by continually trying to elevate my mind and elevate my spirit and care for my body and to be able to love as many people as effectively as possible with this mystery of life that I've been given."

Rule #2: Where You Are Isn't Where You're Going to Be

"We didn't grow up with the sense that, where we were was where we were going to be.

We grew up with the sense that, where we were almost didn't matter, because we were becoming something greater."

Rule #3: Make a Choice *[Evan's Fav]*

"There's a concept that I don't want to be an icon. I want to be an idea. I want to represent an idea. I want to represent possibilities. I want to represent magic. That you're in the universe, and two plus two equals four.

Two plus two only equals four if you accept that two plus two equals four. Two plus two is going to be what I want it to be. And there is a *redemptive power that making a choice has.*

And rather than feeling like you are an effect to all the things that are happening, make a choice. *You just decide what is going to be, who you are going to be, how you are going to do it.*

Just decide. And from that point, *the universe is going to get out of your way.* It's water. It wants to move and go around stuff. So for me, I want to represent possibilities. I want to represent the idea that you really can make what you want.

One of my favorite books is 'The Alchemist', Paulo Coelho. I just believe that. *I believe that I can create whatever I want to create.* If I can put my head on it right, study it, learn the patterns. And it's hard to put it into words, real metaphysical esoteric nonsense. But I feel really strongly that we are who we choose to be."

Rule #4: Have a Purpose

"The difference between depression and joy, I think is purpose. It's like when you wake up in the morning, and your life means something to somebody other than you. That you have a purpose.

If you don't go do the thing that you're going to do, people's lives will suffer. And I think that, that kind of purpose, to live in service, not to you, but to live in service to humanity, to live in service to your family, to live in service to your church, to your city, to your country, to the world.

Living in service. I feel like that is the purest form of joy."

Rule #5: Be Great

"Greatness is not this wonderful, esoteric, elusive, God-like feature that only the special among us will ever taste.

It's something that *truly exists in all of us.*

It's very simple. This is what I believe and I'm willing to die for it. Period. It's that simple.

I know who I am, and that's all I need to know.

So from there, you do what you need to do.

And I think what happens is we make the situation more complex than it has to be."

Rule #6: Don't Chase Money

"I never did anything for money. It was never about money. My experience has been *when people do things for money you make bad choices.*

Find what you love and then you'll learn how to make money doing what you love. When I changed careers, I was never changing to something for money, I was changing to something I loved more.

And that, to me that's really the only way to keep the passion.

If you have two choices, and one is playing the piano and another one is bowling, and you can make more money bowling but you love playing the piano more, *you've got to play the piano.*

You'll tear yourself apart if you're not doing the thing that you love most in life. And you know what it is right now. Right now, there's something that you love more than everything.

Whatever it is that you love crazy, has to *be the thing that you dedicate your life to.*"

Rule #7: Don't Be Outworked

"The only thing that I can see that is distinctly different about me is, I'm not afraid to die on a treadmill. I will run. *I will not be outworked*. Period.

You might have more talent than me, you might be smarter than me, you might be sexier than me. You might be all of those things that you got it on me in nine categories, but if we get on the treadmill together, there is two things: You're getting off first, or I'm going to die. It's really that simple.

So, let's go back to the question about whether people block me out. It's going to be two options: I'm going to get back in, or I'm going to be dead. *You are not going to outwork me.* It's such a simple basic concept.

The guy who is willing to hustle the most is going to be a guy that just gets that loose ball. It's going to be out of bounds but he saved it back in.

It's like the commodity that I see the majority of people who aren't getting the places they want or aren't achieving the things that they want. This business is strictly based on hustle. Strictly based on being outworked. Strictly based on missing crucial opportunities. I say it all the time, *if you stay ready you ain't got to get ready."*

Rule #8: Work On Your Skills

"The *separation of talent and skill* is one of the greatest misunderstood concepts for people who are trying to excel at their dreams. Talent you get naturally. Skill is only developed by hours, and hours, and hours of beating on your craft.

There is no easy way around it. No matter how talented you are, your talent is going to fail you if you are not skilled.

If you don't study, if you don't *work really hard, and dedicate yourself to being better every single day."*

Rule #9: Let Fear Motivate You

"I'm motivated by fear. Fear of fear. I hate being scared to do something. I hate that feeling, the feeling that I had before I had a meeting with Quincy Jones.

It was really Quincy Jones and a guy named Benny Medina, and Jeff Polly that came with the idea for 'The Fresh Prince of Bel-Air.'

And I hated being scared. I didn't want to even take the meeting.

There were opportunities during my first year as a rapper. Bill Cosby and the people in 'The Cosby Show' had seen my music video and called me to come and try out for 'The Cosby Show.'

And just, every time it was set up, for some reason, I couldn't make it.

The fear, I hated, I just hated being scared to do something. And I think what developed in my early days was the *attitude that I started attacking things that I was scared of."*

Rule #10: Focus

"I realize that to have the level of success that I want to have, *it's difficult to spread it out and do multiple things in order to be world class.*

And I made a decision: *I want to be world class.* It takes such a desperate, obsessive focus to excel on a level that I want to make movies.

When I was young, I sat in the movie theater and watched 'Star Wars' and I just couldn't believe that that movie made me feel like that. Just floored and stunned by the creativity.

And I'm realizing that in order to move people in that way, in order to touch people in that way, *you've really got to focus* with all of your fiber and all of your heart and all your creativity."

Will Smith Summary

1. Improve Yourself
2. Where You Are Isn't Where You're Going to Be
3. Make a Choice
4. Have a Purpose
5. Be Great
6. Don't Chase Money
7. Don't be Outworked
8. Work on Your Skills
9. Let Fear Motivate You
10. Focus

How can you apply these rules to your business or life today?

_____

_____

_____

_____

_____

_____

_____

_____

_____

_____

_____

#DidYouKnow: Will Smith had high SAT scores and interest from MIT but never applied to college because he wanted to rap.

"Prepare yourself so that you can be a rainbow in somebody else's clouds. Be a blessing to somebody." – Maya Angelou

- Poet, memoirist, and civil rights activist
- Best known for her series of 7 autobiographies
- Books center on themes of racism, identity, family, and travel
- Made 80 appearances a year as a speaker into her 80s
- Received more than 50 honorary degrees

Rule #1: Just Do Right! *[Evan's Fav]*

"I have a painting by Phoebe of nine women, and they all look like women in my grandmother's prayer meeting group. So, whenever I'm obliged to do something, I take that painting and I look at that painting. There's an *empty chair* and I think, now what would Grandma do? What would she say?

I can almost hear her voice saying, 'Now sister, you know what's right. Just do right.' You don't really have to ask anybody. The truth is, right may not be expedient, it may not be profitable, but it will *satisfy your soul*. It brings you the kind of protection that bodyguards can't give you.

Try to be all you can be to be the best human being you can be. Try to be that in your church, in your temple. Try to be that in your classroom. Do it because it is right to do. You see, people will know you and they will add their prayers to your life. They'll wish you well. If your name is mentioned and people say, 'Oh, hell. Oh, damn,' I think you're doing something wrong. But if your name is mentioned and people say, 'Oh, she's so sweet. He's so nice. Oh, God bless her.' There you are. So *try to live your life in a way that you will not regret years of useless virtue and inertia and timidity.*

Take up the battle, take it up. It's yours. *This is your life.* This is your world. I'll be leaving it long before you under the ordinary set of circumstances. You make your own choices. You can decide life isn't worth living and that would be the worst thing you can do. How do you know so far? Try it. See. So, pick it up. Pick the battle and make it a better world. Just where you are. Yes. And it can be better and it must be better, but it is up to us."

Rule #2: Be Courageous

"*Courage is the most important of all the virtues* because without courage, you can't practice any other virtue consistently. You see? You can't be consistently kind or fair or humane or generous, not without courage because if you don't have it, sooner or later, you'll stop and say, 'Eh, the threat is too much. The difficulty is too high. The challenge is too great.'"

Rule #3: Love Yourself

"I believe that **self-love** is very important. If you read my work, you know I'm always talking about loving oneself. I never trust anybody who tells me he or she loves me if the person doesn't love herself or himself. There's an African saying which is, **'Be careful when a naked person offers you a shirt.'** I mean if he had something, he'd cover himself first, right? So I like to look at self-love.

It is very important that it **comes from within,** that you have a sense of yourself so that when you walk into an office, you don't go alone, bring your people with you. Bring everybody who have loved you with you. Say, 'Grandma, come on. Let's go. Great-Grandpa, you've been dead all this time. Come on. Let's go. I have to have an interview. Come on Auntie. Come on my friends. Come. Let's go.'

And when you walk in, people don't know what it is about you, that can't take their eyes off you. You may not be cute in the given sense. You may not be high-fashion model size in that particular sense. You may not be any of those things, but they can't take their eyes off you. And they say of you, in this incredible way, which I don't understand, they say, 'I don't know, but she has charisma.' No. What you have is all those people around you. So think of that any time you have anything to do.

Bring everybody with you that you can remember who has loved you and then you have that sense of having been paid for and when you walk in people will say now, **'I think you're overqualified.'"**

Rule #4: Laugh

"If you don't laugh, you will die. You know, you really must laugh. And if every human being in the world would admit it, he or she is the funniest person you've ever met. And the truth is some people just rather be a little stodgy and boring but the truth is, they themselves know that they are very funny. The sense of humor isn't in self-defense against those who pretend not to have any sense of humor and against the cruelties of life. One must laugh."

Rule #5: Be a Blessing to Somebody

"There's an African-American song, 19th century, which is so great. It says, *'When it looks like the sun wasn't going to shine anymore God put a rainbow in the clouds.'* I've had so many rainbows in my clouds. I've had a lot of clouds. But I have had so many rainbows. And one of the things I do when I step up on a stage, when I stand up to translate, when I go to teach my classes, when I go to direct a movie, I bring everyone who has ever been kind to me with me. Black, white, Asian, Spanish-speaking, Native American, gay, straight, everybody. I say, 'Come with me. I'm going on the stage. Come with me, I need you now.' So I don't ever feel I have no help. And the thing to do, it seems to me, is to be prepared yourself so that *you can be a rainbow in somebody else's cloud.* Somebody who may not look like you, may not call God the same name you call God, if they call God at all. I may not eat the same dishes prepared the way you do, may not dance your dances or speak your language, but *be a blessing to somebody."*

Rule #6: Turn Struggles Into Triumphs

"When I was seven and a half, I was raped. The rapist was a person well known to my family. I was hospitalized. The rapist was let out of jail and was found dead that night. I thought I had caused the man's death because I had spoken his name. That was my logic. So I stopped talking for five years. Now, to show you again how out of evil there can come good, in those five years, *I read every book* in the black school library. I read all the books I could get from the white school library. I was saved in that muteness. When I decided to speak, I had a lot to say and many ways in which to say what I had to say. I listened to the black minister, I listened to the melody of the preachers, and I could tell when they would start up on that kind of thing when we know they mean to take our souls straight to heaven. I understood it. So out of this evil rape on the body of a young person more often than not introduces cynicism and there's nothing quite so tragic as a young cynic because it means the person has gone from knowing nothing to believing nothing. In my case, I was saved in that muteness. *I was saved and I was able to draw from human thought, human disappointments and triumphs enough to triumph myself."*

Rule #7: Lift People Up

"People will very often try to respond to you on the level on which you address them.

So if you say, 'Aren't you wonderful? Aren't you splendid? My goodness you're beautiful. Oh, you're so bright.'

People will try, even if they're not, they really will try to lift themselves up to that.

On the other hand, if you say, 'You know you're a dog. You really are so low. You'll never be anybody. In fact, you're a nobody now and you never have been.'

Sooner or later, that person will respond on the level on which he or she is addressed.

He will say figuratively or literally 'Let me show you where dog is. Let me show you where low really is. I will show you that.'

Dears, try to **introduce courtesy** into your speech to each other.

You have no idea what it would do for your brother or sister to whom you speak.

And you surely have no idea what it would do for you.

It will lift you up."

Rule #8: Learn to Say 'No'

"There's a place in you that you must keep inviolate. You must keep it pristine, clean so that nobody has the right to curse you, treat you badly. Nobody.

No mother, father, no wife, no husband. Nobody because that may be the place you go to when you meet God. You have to have a place where they just say, 'Stop it. Back up.'"

Rule #9: Always Do Your Best

Interviewer: "When you're writing poetry, are you writing to express your experiences or do you write to inspire other people?"

Maya Angelou: "No, I write to try to say what I see, what I've seen. And of course, I hope that it's inspirational."

Interviewer: "When you were writing 'Phenomenal Woman', did you realize how many millions of women would be inspired by that?"

Maya Angelou: "No. I didn't realize any of that. *I just do the best I can.*"

Rule #10: Keep Rising

"You may write me down in history with your bitter, twisted lies. You may trod me in the very dirt, but still, like dust, I'll rise. Does my sassiness upset you? Why are you beset with gloom? Just because I walk as if I have got oil wells pumping in my living room.

Just like moons and like suns, with the certainty of tides. Just like hopes springing high, still, I rise. Did you want to see me broken? Bowed head and lowered eyes? Shoulders falling down like teardrops, weakened by my soulful cries?

Does my sassiness upset you? Don't you take it so hard just cause I laugh as if I have gold mines digging in my own backyard. *You can shoot me with your words, you may cut me with your lies, you can kill me with your hatefulness, but just like life, I'll rise.*

Does my sexiness offend you? Awww. Does it come as a surprise that I dance as if I have diamonds at the meeting of my thighs? Out of the huts of history's shame, I rise. Up from a past rooted in pain, I rise. A black ocean, leaping and wide, welling and swelling and bearing in the tide. Leaving behind nights of terror and fear, I rise. Into a daybreak miraculously clear, I rise. Bringing the gifts that my ancestors gave, I am the hope and the dream of the slave. And so, there I go."

Maya Angelou Summary

1. Just Do Right!
2. Be Courageous
3. Love Yourself
4. Laugh
5. Be a Blessing to Somebody
6. Turn Struggles Into Triumphs
7. Lift People Up
8. Learn to Say 'No'
9. Always Do Your Best
10. Keep Rising

How can you apply these rules to your business or life today?

_____

_____

_____

_____

_____

_____

_____

_____

_____

_____

_____

#DidYouKnow: Maya Angelou was active in the Civil Rights Movement and worked with Martin Luther King Jr. and Malcolm X.

"If you become vocal with it, you're creating that law of attraction and it will become reality." – Conor McGregor

- Mixed martial artist and UFC Champion
- Began boxing when he was 12 years old
- Competed as a featherweight, lightweight, and welterweight
- 1st UFC fighter with titles in 2 weight classes simultaneously
- Known for being the biggest pay-per-view draw in MMA

Rule #1: Love What You Do *[Evan's Fav]*

"I'm just curious about it. It's in my head 24/7. There's nothing else I can think. I don't think about nothing else.

That's it, I'm just curious. Everything I do in my life is related to this. I don't do nothing else if it's not got to do with fighting. Know what I mean? That is why. To be truthful, all you got to do is show up.

I'm in phenomenal shape in body and mind. To me, what's unhealthy is living an unhealthy life.

To me, *what's unhealthy is getting up and going through the same day every day of your life 9 to 5 in an office.*

That's unhealthy. That beats your mind.

I don't work. *I love what I do and that's why I'm doing what I love.* And that's why it's become a career for me, because I love it. I love what I do so I don't think it's unhealthy. I feel good in my mind. It's my life."

Rule #2: Carry On

"You stare at your past and you'll end up staying there. It's okay to look back and admire it, but you carry on. I'm not in the business of staring back at it and getting lost back there.

People say a loss can make or break a fighter, but trust me, a win can also make or break a fighter because they get comfortable with a win.

People can get comfortable with a win and slack off then. Slack off on the training. Slack off on the diet. They've won one, they're winners now.

That's not me. *You sleep on a win and you wake up with a loss,* so I just carry on, keep doing what I'm doing. It's perfect. Continue on this path. The freight train straight to the top."

Rule #3: Have Courage to Speak Up

"If you can see it here and you have the courage enough to speak it, it will happen.

So, I see these shots, I see these sequences, and I don't shy away from them.

A lot of times people believe in certain things, but they keep to themselves. They don't put it out there.

If you truly *believe in it, if you become vocal with it, you're creating that law of attraction and it will become reality."*

Rule #4: Create Your Own Path

"I was thrown into a plumbing trade.

Didn't give a sh** about plumbing, didn't know anything about plumbing.

I just went on that site because *culture told me that that's what I have to do.*

I did it for a while and then I realized this is not what I want to do. If this is not what I want to do, then what the f*** am I doing it for?

And I walked out, 18 months in maybe.

Earlier on, obviously I didn't know what it was.

I couldn't look to my mother and say, 'Hey, this Irish man did it. I'm going to follow in this footsteps,' because there were no footsteps.

I had to create my own footsteps and follow them. They were a little unsure at first but they supported me and they knew I would do it. If I said I would do it, then I would do it."

Rule #5: Prove Them Wrong

"The Irish thing is to get into a trade straightaway. I was no different. As soon as I finished school I was always getting pestered. 'What are you doing with your life?' You know? Doing this, doing that. They didn't know what it was. They didn't know what MMA was. They didn't know none of this. They didn't know I could make a career out of it. As far as they were concerned, mom and dad I'm talking about, I was just getting into a cage and fighting with some other guy. They didn't know nothing about it. No one did, really, but I knew. I knew and then I ended up getting a trade just to keep them quiet because I used to have a lot of fights with me dad. A lot. I ended up getting a trade as a plumber. I used to go up there six o'clock, five o'clock in the morning. Usually 14 hour days. I was like, 'This isn't for me. This is not for me.' I lasted 18 months doing it, but it was tough. It wasn't the life for me. And then John got in touch and says, 'I have a show. On the show would you like to fight on it?' And that was it. I just packed it in, didn't show up. Me dad used to come in and punch the hell out me and try to drag me out of bed and I just wouldn't go. I just packed it in, quit, and then focused on training. I knew what was going to happen. I knew I was going to get here, they didn't. It was a lot of stressful years. A lot of tough times, **but I proved them wrong. I proved myself right.**"

Rule #6: Think Outside the Box

"Every gym I went to had their set way of doing things. Don't do it this way, do it that way. I thought people just had their own set way and you must do it that way. You must stand this way. You must kick this way. You must punch this way. I met my coach, John Kavanagh, it wasn't like that. He had a more open mind and he encouraged different movements. I'd never experienced that before. I'd never heard a coach say that to me before. That stuck in my head and I talked to him. And I said, *'This guy is thinking outside the box.'* He has a vision that everything works and he encourages every movement because ultimately there is a time and a place for every single move. So, I just knew when I met John and when he spoke it made complete sense to me and that was it. I stuck with him and he stuck with me and the rest is history."

Rule #7: Be Grateful

"Gratitude is one of the strongest forms of power in attracting good things. If you truly feel grateful for the things in your life. I always felt grateful for even the small things. I always used to celebrate the small things. Now I might be celebrating the bigger things, but I always celebrate every little good thing that would happen to me in my life even before I had any kind of money or any of that. I would celebrate and I would feel grateful for it.

And it just gave me more and this is exactly the same thing that's happening right now. I still remain grateful and more comes."

Rule #8: Have Heroes

"Of course I am familiar with Muhammad Ali. You don't just have him here, he is global. He is the man. Muhammad Ali was a guy that has done what had not been done before. Change, not only the face of his game, but the face of the world. He was outspoken. He fought for what he believed in. He was charismatic. *He was a legend, a hero,* and I looked up to him. One of my first heroes was Muhammad Ali.

When I was 11 years old there was a group of people and they tried to attack me and a fight broke out and it was just me and one guy before everyone else jumped in on me, but we were fighting each other. And I slipped a punch and I shuffled my shoulders and said, 'Muhammad Ali!' And threw a shot. And he rolled under the shot but fell into a knee and I ended up on top of him. So, I'm out there calling myself Muhammad Ali and I'm punching him in the head. Then somebody came in and tried to kick me and then a whole group of them came in and it was just a big fight, but it was me against six of them. And I ended up getting my ass whooped.

I done the Ali shuffle. I'm only 11 years old. I done the Ali shuffle, threw a left hook. He rolled under the left hook. It was good of him to roll. He saw it coming and rolled under it, but he rolled right into a knee. I was prepared. I was studying tape, so definitely Muhammad Ali was a hero of mine."

Rule #9: Live Everyday Like a Champion

"I don't like thinking too far ahead. People set goals, long distance goals. That's too much for me. I already feel like I'm living it and then I just carry on. *I carry on day by day already living the final goal,* the goal of being the world champion. I already carry myself like I'm a world champion.

I already speak like I'm a world champion and that's it. I just carry on day by day so I'll take it as it comes.

Again, like I said, you're asking me about the future. I'll let you know a little bit closer.

All I can see right now is the gold. That's all I can see."

Rule #10: Train in Martial Arts

"There's parents coming in with their kids bringing them into the gym. Their mom and dad by their side, encouraging it. I was never like that. That's going to go to the next level when you have the parents encouraging the dream.

People can say it's barbaric and martial arts is barbaric, or this game is too much. It's two men beating each other or whatever. *The martial arts life will give you a discipline, will give you a dedication, will give you a drive that you won't get nowhere else.*

Whatever these kids that come in at that size with their parents, whatever they decide to do, whether they decide to conquer the martial arts world, the fighting game, or whether they want to go and conquer the business world.

Whatever they decide to do, training for combat sport, training martial arts will give them that *confidence to go and excel in anything.*

People can criticize about it all they want but the results speak for themselves. And seeing these little kids coming in this size, it's good times, good times ahead I see."

Conor McGregor Summary

1. Love What You Do
2. Carry On
3. Have Courage to Speak Up
4. Create Your Own Path
5. Prove Them Wrong
6. Think Outside the Box
7. Be Grateful
8. Have Heroes
9. Live Everyday Like a Champion
10. Train in Martial Arts

How can you apply these rules to your business or life today?

_____

_____

_____

_____

_____

_____

_____

_____

_____

_____

_____

_____

#DidYouKnow: Conor McGregor does not have any pre-fight rituals because he believes them to be "a form of fear."

"The more people you reach the more people are going to think that you suck. You can't please everybody." – Louis C.K.

- Comedian, actor, writer, producer, director, and editor
- Creator, executive producer, and star of the FX series Louie
- Considered one of the greatest stand-up comics of all time
- Has won a 2012 Peabody Award and 6 Emmy awards
- His album Live at Madison Square Garden won a Grammy

Rule #1: Keep Pushing

"So I've tried TV. I try it and it doesn't work and then I go back to comedy. And if something I'm doing as a standup leads me back to like, 'Hey this might be a show,' then I'll try. I'll try anything that I think might be good. I don't care about, 'Well I failed at it before.' **Who cares? Try it again.** The very first time I got a deal to do a pilot for a sitcom, I wrote it and they really liked it and it got close, and then they said we're not going to make the pilot. Then, I wrote Saint Louie and they made the pilot. We got to shoot a pilot. It was so exciting and then they said, 'We're not going to make the show.' All right. Third time around, made a pilot, and got one season of 'Lucky Louie' on the air. And then that's all they wanted. I did one season. Okay. And now I've done 'Louie,' and it's gone three seasons. So I got a little further each time. I pushed the ball a little further ahead each time. I mean, not doing something because it didn't work would be like if you're a quarterback and you go the line of scrimmage at the 25 and you hand the ball off and the guy pushes it eight yards and you're like, well we didn't score a touchdown, so I'll go home. **You keep pushing.**"

Rule #2: You Can't Please Everybody

"15,000 people laughing at your jokes, that's kind of an amazing feeling. But also having them sit there looking at you listening is really great too. But I always see, I've done it three times now and it was the same every time that they're all laughing, the show's going great, but what I see are there's at least, in 15,000 people, there's like a thousand disappointed people. There's like a thousand people.

And they're dotted. I see them all. I see them still today. But during the show, I see them, just guys going like, 'Ehh.' Those are the ones that you really see. Everyone's going, 'Yay!' And I'm just, 'Ah, I'm sorry buddy.'

The more people you reach and the more people that see you, the more people are going to think that you suck. That's just the law of mathematics. **You can't please everybody.**"

Rule #3: Always Try to Improve *[Evan's Fav]*

"It's about doing the best show that you can do and it's about *staying at the edge.*

I want to do a better show every time I'm on stage.

Part of it is that I want what I *do to keep getting better.*

I think a lot of people in show business and comedy especially are very lazy and they just sort of think that you just get up there and then you wait for your manager to get you a better one. A better shot.

But it's something you've got to *really keep working at.* I wouldn't like it if I stopped trying really hard. It isn't a neurosis, like 'Oh geez, I hope they like me.'

This is what I do, I've got to do it really well."

Rule #4: Don't Waste Time

"I grew up when I had kids and started really thinking about standup. When I had kids, it made a big difference for me because when I went out to do a set, it wasn't a social event.

It was until that point, you just go to the Comedy Cellar, have a falafel at the comedy table, run down and do your set, bull with some comics. It was a lot of wasting time.

And it didn't really matter how the set was, that was just the job. I'm just going to go on and do my time, tell the same jokes, maybe do one new joke. But now it's like, I got kids and getting out of the house is a big deal.

I can do a set tonight and I *ain't wasting any time.* I got a list of stuff I want to try. I want to make sure that this set makes me better. I started to think every set I do has to make me a better comic."

Rule #5: Welcome Obstacles

"Some resistance is always good for art I think. Michelangelo has this big block of marble and he needs to dig David out of there, right? Not only does he need to chip away just the right amount of marble but he has to then find this thing in there and then he has to smooth that out make it perfect .

If Michelangelo was given marble and David just comes away, would he have been a better sculptor? You know what I mean? There's something about the having to navigate. Just being like, 'I don't think I can do this.' *I think it's a great push for an artist.* This is going to be impossible. I think sometimes it can sharpen your vision."

Rule #6: Survive Failure

"'I wrote and directed 'Pootie Tang'. I had already shot it and it was during the editing process. I got flown out to L.A.. I have no idea. Well, I kind of smelled something, but they took me to Paramount. And I went to John Goldwyn's office. He was Samuel Goldwyn's grandson. And so I'm in his office. I'm in the most important office at Paramount. He was running the studio at the time.

I remember I walked in and he's shaking a little because he's so mad. Everybody was there that was involved in the movie. He just unloaded on me and said, 'This movie is unreleasable! You have wasted my money! This is irresponsible. I have a problem with everyone here!' And then this guy who was the President of M.T.V. Films said, 'Well John, I don't think you really got the film.' 'How dare you say that to me!'

I'll never forget that moment. Because all I wanted to do is make movies at the time and it was being destroyed by Samuel Goldwyn's grandson. And I'm sitting there, but a part of me was outside of my body going, *'You are in the Paramount big office being yelled at. How cool is this?' I was able to enjoy it.* Who gets to have that very rare, beautiful experience to get to heaven? To me, the key is surviving failure. It's a very great experience to have."

Rule #7: Learn Your Business

"There are some people who like to just show up and do a show and get a check. I'm interested in everything. When I tour and they tell me, 'Hey you're doing the Chicago Theater and here's how much you're making,' they tell me this big exciting number. Then I go, I ask them, 'Well how much are the tickets?' And then they go 'Well, in order to pay you that they're charging 50 bucks a ticket.' 'I don't want people to pay 50 bucks a ticket to see me. How much do I get paid if they pay 30 bucks a ticket?' 'Well geez, it's only this.' And I'm like, 'Well that's more money than my dad made in his life. I mean, I'll take it.' Once I started looking at it that way, I learned stuff. I learned that if you ask for a high guarantee for a live show, you drive up the ticket price because the risk is higher. But if you tell the theater, 'Look, don't guarantee me anything. **Only pay me if we make money.'** Then the price of the tickets come down and they don't have to advertise as much because they're not as afraid that they're going to lose. If you work in a theater without a guarantee, you actually get paid more because the show costs less. It costs less for the advertising, all that stuff. So if you sell it out, you will make more money. So I started learning about that."

Rule #8: Be Calm

"Like the story I tell on 'Conan' about the guy next to me on the airplane when the Internet shuts down suddenly. I was really upset that the Internet shut down. I was livid.

And then I caught myself and said, 'Wait a minute. What are you upset about? This was incredible that this was possible even. It was kind of like an epiphany for me. I started seeing things differently, like realizing that when we get to a gate and they go, 'We need ten minutes because the plane at our gate hasn't backed out yet.' And I go, 'Okay, come on!' That was me. 'Let's go!' Why? It's actually not going to get me there quicker. **I'm losing nothing.** I just feel bad. But if you can just **take a breath and calm down** and go, 'You know this is as good as they make these right now. This is as good as it is. And it's pretty goddamned great.' But somehow, we don't. Part of me feels like that if people have to go back to basics a little bit."

Rule #9: Use Pressure to Motivate You

"I'm terrified of tapping out. But that's a motivating fear. That's pressure. I like pressure. I learned that from Billie Jean King, one of my heroes. I remember as a kid watching a press conference with Billie Jean King and Bobby Riggs when they were doing 'Battle of the Sexes.' I was raised by a single mom and I have three older sisters so I've always identified with women and I never saw women as weak. I only ever knew my strong working single mother. So watching Billie Jean King was fascinating because of the way she carried it. That's what made it work. Because he would sit there going, 'Why don't you all get back in the kitchen?' And the way she carried it was amazing. She didn't sit there and turn red and get angry. She just sat there and then they asked her, 'How do you feel when he says all this?' And she smiled and she said, 'All it does is put a lot of pressure on me. And I love pressure.' And she had this big smile on her face. She said I love pressure. And I thought, 'Oh my God. How do you love... what does that mean?' I thought really carefully about that. She was like, 'Come on, keep it coming. I love it. I love it. I want this pressure.' She knows how to turn pressure into hard work. It motivates her. So she's like, 'Go ahead.' The more he said the more she had to win. She had so much to lose that she knew *she'd play better. So that's the way I do it. It pushes me."*

Rule #10: Appreciate Life

"Life is short. Life is very short. I like life. I like it. I feel like even if it ends up being short, I got lucky to have it cause life is an amazing gift when you think about what you get with a basic life. Not even a particularly lucky life or a healthy life. If you have a life you get to be on Earth. First of all, oh my God, what a location! This is Earth and for trillions of miles in every direction, it sucks so bad. It's so bad that your eyes bolt out of your head cause it sucks so bad. You get to be on Earth and as long as you're not blind or whatever, you get to be here, you get to eat food. You get to put bacon in your mouth. I mean when you have bacon in your mouth, it doesn't matter who's President. You just, 'Ahhhh. Ahhhhh.' Every time I'm eating bacon, I think, I could die right now and I mean it. That's how good life is."*

Louis C.K. Summary

1. Keep Pushing
2. You Can't Please Everybody
3. Always Try to Improve
4. Don't Waste Time
5. Welcome Obstacles
6. Survive Failure
7. Learn Your Business
8. Be Calm
9. Use Pressure to Motivate You
10. Appreciate Life

How can you apply these rules to your business or life today?

_____

_____

_____

_____

_____

_____

_____

_____

_____

_____

_____

_____

#DidYouKnow: In 2011, Louis C.K. made $1,000,000 in a matter of days, half of which he gave to his staff and charities.

"You have to love what you do. It solves a lot of problems. When you love what you do you, you work harder." – Donald Trump

- 45th President of the United States, entrepreneur
- The oldest and wealthiest person ever to become President
- Time named him Person of the Year in 2016
- Has a star on the Hollywood Walk of Fame
- Made cameo appearances in 12 films and 14 TV series

Rule #1: Don't Do it for the Money

"I love the game.

I like the money and the money is certainly a method of keeping score, but I don't do things for money.

I do things because I enjoy doing them.

That really can sometimes translate into more money than you would have made if you weren't just after the money."

Rule #2: Never Give Up

"Never, ever give up.

You can change and you can move around but never ever give up. I know people that are very smart.

They went to the Wharton School of Finance with me.

I know other people that aren't as smart and those people are the top people in the industry today and *they just were tougher.*

They didn't give up.

And the smart ones had everything on their plate.

They'd always come in with the A plus on the tests and the good boards and everything else.

But when they ran into problems, they did not know how to solve the problems like the guys that weren't as good.

And it's very seldom that you see something other than this happen.

So never, ever give up."

Rule #3: Be Into the Details

"A lot of that is all in the details. You've got to be into the details because if you're not they'll come back to haunt you.

So often, life is in the details. Well business is also in the details.

You have to be very careful, you have to watch the dotted i's because you can really lose tremendously if you don't watch those details.

It's all about the details. That's very important."

Rule #4: Be Totally Focused

"You want to be totally focused. You can't take your eye off the ball.

When I had troubles in the early 90's, a major article came out and it said very strongly, 'Everything he touches turns to gold.'

And I believed it. So I would go out with models that night instead of working, but that wasn't good.

And I remember, I had a big lease coming up, there was a big show, and I went to the show.

I said, don't worry fellas, you can handle the lease, you'll get it done. Well I came back, they didn't get it done, and I would have had it done 100%.

And then the market crashed in the 90's, so I had trouble, but it was sort of amazing.

I wouldn't want to do it again but it was amazing test of yourself.

Can you handle pressure? How are you under pressure? Are you smart? You know, when everybody's coming at you."

Rule #5: Get Great Employees

"The worst employee is a good employee. A bad employee is fine because you fire that person right away.

A great employee is phenomenal. You want to keep them and cherish them. They're fantastic.

But a good employee, you never sort of fire them. But they never lead you to the next level. They just keep their job. They're sort of too good to be fired, but they're not good enough.

You're never going to do great. So I always say, the worst employee isn't a bad employee. It's just a **good or average employee.***

Rule #6: Work Hard

"Gary Player, the great golfer, he was a little guy, very little, but he worked really hard and he had a great statement.

He'd go, *'The harder I work, the luckier I get.'* And he wins the US Open.

You have all these big handsome guys, these big giant guys, and they'd hit the ball a mile, and you have Gary Player.

And Gary Player would win the Open. He would win the Masters. He would win this, he'd win that.

In the US Open he hit a five iron to one foot from the hole and he ended up getting a birdie and wins the US Open right.

And he came off the green, and I know I've heard this statement before, but I heard it from him in a meaningful way.

They said, 'What do you think Gary, what is it?' He said, 'All I know is I've been working very hard and **the harder I work, the luckier I get.'** I thought it was an amazing saying."

Rule #7: Change Your Mindset

"I have a friend who was not successful at all, but was really up-and-coming, and he had a thing: He would only fly first class.

I'm not saying do this, because for some people it won't work, but he needed that mentally.

He wanted to fly first class, because mentally, he wanted to think he was the best, and that's it.

And, even though he didn't have much money at the time, this is years ago, he would always fly first class.

I used to criticize him. But it put him in a good state of mind, and he became a very, very successful guy. Very, very successful. And, I've always remembered that.

He would never fly coach. He would always fly first class, even though he didn't have the means to fly."

Rule #8: #Believe in Yourself *[Evan's Fav]*

"So much of success is seeing yourself as victorious.

You have to see yourself, you have to really believe in yourself. And sometimes it's hard.

You've had failures, you've had weaknesses, you've had other things. You have to see yourself as a one man band.

Don't rely too much on other people because they'll let you down.

You have to see yourself as victorious.

And to be a winner you have to think like a winner.

If you don't think like a winner, it's just never going to happen."

Rule #9: Follow Your Instincts

"Sometimes in life to be successful, often times, most of the time, you have to follow your instincts. **You have to follow your gut.** You have to. Your parents may say wrong. Your whomever may say wrong. But you have to do it."

Rule #10: Love What You Do

"You have to love what you do. It solves a lot of problems, because when you love what you do, when you really love what you do, you work harder. I tell this story, a Wall Street type, big guy. He has a son. So he wants his son Alex to go into the firm, of course. And in the meantime, all these kids are graduating from Wharton and Harvard and Stanford and they're just eating Alex's lunch. He doesn't have a chance and he doesn't like it. He's not liking what he's doing. **You've got to love what you do.** So one day I actually told him, 'Why don't you leave? Your father's brutal!' The father's just killing the guy telling him you don't have what it takes. 'You got to leave him.' He said, 'I just can't Donald.'

So anyway he's a member of a very good golf club in Westchester and they put him in charge of doing this big renovation of the course. It's a very good club and he's there every morning at five in the morning. He doesn't leave. He did such an unbelievable job. The contractors respected him, everybody respected him. And they give him an honor. And this is a tough group of people that have this club. The club came in under budget, faster by two months. He did an unbelievable job and the quality of the work was ten times what they ever anticipated. So they gave him a medal.

I said, 'You know, Alex, if you were to go and do this for a living, you ought to be a builder. Whether it's houses, or clubs, or golf courses, renovations or this.' 'Oh my father would go crazy, he'd never let me.' So Alex went back to Wall Street where he was miserable. And a year later, he quit. And he started doing renovations of houses and clubs and different things, and he's doing great. You've got to love what you do."

Donald Trump Summary

1. Don't Do it for the Money
2. Never Give Up
3. Be Into the Details
4. Be Totally Focused
5. Get Great Employees
6. Work Hard
7. Change Your Mindset
8. #Believe in Yourself
9. Follow Your Instincts
10. Love What You Do

How can you apply these rules to your business or life today?

_____

_____

_____

_____

_____

_____

_____

_____

_____

_____

_____

_____

#DidYouKnow: Donald Trump is a World Wrestling Entertainment fan and hosted Wrestlemania IV and V.

"Now is the time to take risk. Do something bold! You won't regret it." – Elon Musk

- Entrepreneur, CEO of SpaceX and Tesla Motors
- His goals revolve around changing the world and humanity
- SpaceX is the largest private maker of rocket motors globally
- One of the Forbes' World's Most Powerful People
- Wants to lower global warming and make life multiplanetary

Rule #1: Expect to Fail

"When you're building something new, there's going to be mistakes, and it's important to recognize those mistakes, acknowledge them, and take corrective action.

The success of a company is very much more about 'How quickly are you to fix the mistakes?' Not, 'Will you make mistakes?'

The difference between a start-up that is successful and one that is not, is because *they've both made of mistakes,* but the successful one recognized the mistakes, fixed them very quickly, and the unsuccessful one tries to deny that the mistakes exist.

In physics, you're taught to always question yourself. You're taught to always assume that you're wrong, not to assume that you're right.

You have to prove yourself not wrong.

I think that physics framework is really where I learnt it and it's very effective for learning counter-intuitive things that aren't obvious.

It's not like I like failure. I mean, who likes failure?

But if you only do things that are certain to succeed, *then you're only going to be doing very obvious things."*

Rule #2: Never Give Up *[Evan's Fav]*

Interviewer: "That *third failure in a row,* did you think, 'I need to pack this in?'

Elon Musk: "Never."

Interviewer: "Why not?"

Elon Musk: *"I don't ever give up.* I have to be dead or completely incapacitated."

Rule #3: Really Like What You Do

"Really liking what you do, whatever area that you get into.

Given that even if you're the best there's always a chance of failure.

So I think it's important that you really like whatever you're doing.

If you don't like it, **life is too short.**

If you like what you're doing, you think about it even when you're not working.

I mean it's something that your mind is drawn to.

And if you don't like it, you just really can't make it work."

Rule #4: Take a Risk

"Now is the time to take risk.

You don't have kids and as you get older your obligations increase.

And once you have a family you start taking risks not just for yourself, but for your family as well.

It gets much harder to do things that might not work out.

So now is the time to do that.

Before you have those obligations.

So I would encourage you to take risks now.

Do something bold!

You won't regret it."

Rule #5: Do Something Important

Reporter: "How did you figure you were going to start a car company and be successful at it?"

Elon Musk: "Well, I didn't really think Tesla would be successful. I thought we'd most likely fail. But I thought that we at least could address the false perception that people had, that an electric car had to be ugly and slow and boring, like a golf cart."

Reporter: "But you say you didn't expect the company to be successful? Then why try?"

Elon Musk: *"If something's important enough, you should try even if the probable outcome is failure."*

Rule #6: Focus On Signal Over Noise

"We focus on signal over noise.

A lot of companies get confused. They spend money on things that don't actually make the product better.

For example, at Tesla, **we've never spent any money on advertising.**

We've put all the money into R&D, and manufacturing and design, to try to make the car as good as possible.

I think that's the way to go.

For any given company just keep thinking about, 'Are all these efforts that people are expending, **are they resulting in a better product or service?'**

And if they're not, stop those efforts."

Rule #7: Look for Problem Solvers

"When I interview someone to work at the companies, I ask them to tell me about the problems they worked on and **how they solved them.**

And if someone was really the person that solved it, they'll be able to answer multiple levels.

They'll be able to go down to the brass tacks and if they won't they'll get stuck.

And then you can say, 'Oh, this person was not really the person who solved it' because **anyone who struggles hard with a problem never forgets it."**

Rule #8: Attract Great People

"If you're creating a company or if you're joining a company, the most important thing is to **attract great people.**

Either join a group that's amazing, that you really respect, or if you're building a company you've got to gather great people.

I mean all a company is, is a group of people that have gathered together to create a product or service.

And depending upon how talented and hard-working that group is, and the degree to which they're focused, cohesively in a good direction, **that will determine the success of the company.**

So, do everything you can to gather great people if you're creating a company."

Rule #9: Have a Great Product

"You have to make sure that whatever you're doing is a **great product or service, it has to be really great.** If you're a new company, I mean unless it's like some new industry or new market that if it's an untapped market, then the standard is lower for your product or service.

But if you're entering anything where there's an existing marketplace against large, entrenched, competitors then, your product or service needs to be **much better than theirs.**

It can't be a little bit better because then you put yourself in the shoes of the consumer, and they say, 'Why would you buy it?' You're always going to buy the trusted brand, **unless there's a big difference.**

So, a lot of times, an entrepreneur will come up with something which is only slightly better, and it can't just be slightly better, it's **got to be a lot better."**

Rule #10: Work Super Hard

"Depending on how well you want to do, and particularly if you're starting a company, **you need to work super hard.** So, what does 'super hard' mean? Well, when my brother and I were starting our first company, instead of getting an apartment we just rented a small office, and we slept on the couch.

We showered at the YMCA. And we were so hard up we had one computer, so, the website was up during the day, and I was coding at night, seven days a week, all the time. I briefly had a girlfriend in that period and, in order to be with me, she had to sleep in the office.

So **we're working every waking hour,** that's the thing I would say. Particularly if you're starting a company. If you do the simple math, if somebody else is working 50 hours, and you're working 100, you'll get twice as much done in the course of a year as the other company."

Elon Musk Summary

1. Expect to Fail
2. Never Give Up
3. Really Like What You Do
4. Take a Risk
5. Do Something Important
6. Focus on Signal over Noise
7. Look for Problem Solvers
8. Attract Great People
9. Have a Great Product
10.   Work Super Hard

How can you apply these rules to your business or life today?

_____

_____

_____

_____

_____

_____

_____

_____

_____

_____

#DidYouKnow: Elon Musk attended the Burning Man festival in 2004 and said he first thought up the idea for SolarCity at the festival.

"Sales is the transference of emotion. And the emotion you're transferring is the emotion of certainty." – Jordan Belfort

- Author, motivational speaker, and former stockbroker
- The Wolf of Wall Street was his memoir turned into a film
- Before college, he made $20,000 selling ice at a local beach
- Built Stratton Oakmont as a franchise of Stratton Securities
- Runs sales seminars focused on sales psychology

Rule #1: Take Action

"I read this book, 'The Secret.' Go into your house, into a quiet room. And you close the lights, draw the shades, and sit on a couch and visualize a big fat check. 25 thousand bucks US, with your name on it. And I want you to imagine that check, and just make that check go bigger in your mind, and make it real, more real, and just, put it out into the ether of the universe and law of attraction will take hold. Just think about it. Hello? If that's your strategy for success, the only thing that will show up in your mailbox, is not the check, it's the fricking eviction notice from your landlord. They'll be towing away your car and you'll be still saying, 'Where's the check, where's the check?' Do I believe in manifestation? Yeah, damn straight I do, but **you've got to take action.** I tried it, I really did, I swear I tried it. So I sat down, I prayed for the check. It never came. But I went out and started taking action, guess what? The check came with an extra couple of zeros."

Rule #2: Learn To Sell

"If you can't sell, if you can't influence, if you can't persuade, good luck trying to get your business off the ground. I'm not talking about just your customers. I'm talking about the bankers, the people of venture capitalists, your vendors, your credit card processor, the people who work for you. At the highest level, what **sales really is, is the transference of emotion.** And the emotion you're transferring is this **emotion of certainty.** That someone feels certain, yeah it's a good thing, it's going to help me, it's going to fill my need. When you're recruiting people, well you're selling people on your vision for the future, your vision for this company. And if you can't do that, good luck trying to get great people to work for you. It cuts to everything. You always see the people they say, 'Oh, he's a visionary.' Well, that's true. But typically not only are they visionaries, they also possess the ability **to sell the vision to other people.** You need to learn how to influence. How about trying to get your kids to make their bed, or do their homework, or believe in the value of education? How about trying to get a landlord to give you a reduction on your rent, or to extend the lease the way you want? How about trying to negotiate terms? It cuts to everything."

Rule #3: Become Unconsciously Competent

"There are four levels of learning. The first is being **unconsciously incompetent.** When you first start doing something you know so little about it, you basically know nothing. The next level is becoming **consciously incompetent.** That means that you're like, 'Jesus Christ, I don't know anything.' You're like, 'There's this, there's that, there's that, there's all these strategies. They all sound great. I don't know them.' That's the next level. Next level above that is called being **consciously competent.** Consciously competent means that you're good at something, but you can't really do it with your eyes closed yet. You're good, but it requires all your focus and your mental energy. You can't tie your shoe and have a conversation at the same time. That's when you're consciously competent in something. It requires all your conscious focus. The next level above that is called being **unconsciously competent.** And that means when you're really, really great at something, you can do it without thinking about it. And the only way to get from conscious competence, to unconscious competence is through practice. There's no other way. By drilling it into your head, again, and again, and again, and again, and again, until your brain just clicks, and all of a sudden you're using the unconscious part of your mind, which is infinitely more powerful than your conscious mind."

Rule #4: Set Your Goals High

"The reason that most people are not successful, or not wealthy, is not because they set their goals too high and miss them. **It's because they set them too low and hit them.** And you get caught up in the average daily struggle of averages and mediocrity. The idea here is: You want to set the goals just above your comfort zone. Think about your goals right now. How do you set them? Are you setting them very low and hitting them? Are you setting goals that don't inspire you? They're not the sort of goals that make you jump out of bed in the morning, make you want to go to work for yourself. To secure the future, not just for you, but for your family. So you don't have to compromise or acquiesce to anybody, unless you love them, unless you want to. **That's freedom.** Money's just a mechanism to get there."

Rule #5: Have a Vision

"Most people don't have a compelling vision for their own future. They don't. They move through life setting goals, and goals have no power. I believe in setting goals, but there's got to be *something above your goals.* And that's your vision. It's about the world being a certain way. When you truly have a vision for your future that inspires you, you're going to jump up out of bed in the morning, and feel great about going at life, versus being miserable, and going to a job you hate, or living a life that doesn't empower you, and just every day moving through just almost like an automaton, not really having the zest, and the grit, and the greatness of life. Once you become conscious of that, you can create a vision for your future, you write it down. And when you finally hit on it, you know how you know you got it? When you read it back to yourself, your vision statement, and it moves you, and you feel inspired. Every human being is thirsty for a vision. And so few people have it. And so what do they do? They gravitate toward someone who has a vision for the future, because they want to be a part of a vision. *Being a great entrepreneur is being able to create the vision, and then sell that vision to other people."*

Rule #6: Be Honest With Yourself

"The only thing that stops you from getting what you want in life is the bullsh** story you tell yourself of why you can't have it. Because the story stops you from getting honest. And if you can't get honest with yourself, there's nowhere you can go. Imagine like this, success in sales and life, it's like a road map. You know where you want to go and you have this perfect strategy with a straight line to get there. It's a perfect strategy. It's going to get you there every single time. But if you don't know your starting point, if you're not getting honest with where you actually are, it doesn't matter how powerful the strategy is, and it doesn't matter how powerful your goal is. There are three things that you need to know. *Where you are, where you want to go, and how you're going to get there.* Those are the three things you must have to take advantage of any opportunity. You've got to get honest. Don't blame the boss, don't blame the leagues, don't blame your job, don't blame the industry you're in. *Just get honest."*

Rule #7: Get Rich Quick

"My message is this: There's only one way to get rich, and that's quick. That's not a get rich quick scheme, though. Because the **world's too expensive to get rich slowly.**

What I mean by getting rich quick is that there are certain things you have to know. On the inner game of wealth: How you **manage your emotional state, your beliefs, your standards, your focus.** Then on the outer game: Entrepreneurship, sales, marketing, how to develop multiple streams of income.

A lot of hard work goes into getting this lined up but once you have it all lined up and you've done the work, then you can make money very, very quickly.

So it's not a scheme, but you've got to get rich quick and you have to put the work in. I say, if you don't want to work hard, good luck. I don't know any rich people that don't work really, really hard. That's the bottom line.

Before the money starts pouring in. That's the distinction that I think a lot of people who are not wealthy, they don't get that. They think that you accumulate money a little bit at a time, it doesn't work that way. **You work, work, work, work,** don't get the result, bam, one last piece of the puzzle clicks in.

And it all happens quickly."

Rule #8: Master Your Internal World

"Take a **longer term view.** Not just to look three months from now, but look three years from now. The future's going to come, whether you like it or not, so you want to be one step ahead.

It's psychology. Everything, again life, most of life, comes down to psychology. It starts here, in the internal world. **Before you can master the external world, you have to master your own internal world.** That's the true secret to success."

Rule #9: Try Your Hardest

"My son's 14 and we're having this conversation about when he plays in sports about do you *go full out,* or do you not. And I see sometimes in him that when he's out on the field he doesn't play full out, and will have an excuse like, 'My leg hurts,' or 'My arm hurts.' Or something happened. The coach was unfair. The referee was unfair. And what happens with people is we tend to go out into the world and we look for those sort of excuses about why things aren't the way we want them. And when you do that, you lose all your power in life. *When you start focusing on the external, on the excuses, you lose your power."*

Rule #10: Create Your Destiny *[Evan's Fav]*

"Poor people believe they are creatures of circumstance. That means that life happens to them. Rich people are creators of circumstance. *There is no more destructive belief in the world than to think that life happens to you.* The first thing you do is you play the blame game. You start blaming everybody for why you don't have what you want. You'll blame the government, you'll blame your family, you'll blame your spouse, you'll blame your boss, you'll blame the economy, you'll blame the people on Wall Street, which probably deserves some blame. But you'll blame anybody and everybody when you think the world happens to you. You're powerless. That's what complaining does.

The second thing you do, is you *justify.* It's because, because the economy stinks. It's because people are unfair to me. It's because money doesn't really matter anyway.

Third. This is the worst one of all. They *complain.* I hate these people. What you focus on expands, gets bigger. And what you focus on, you attract, because you move towards it. So here's what happens. When you're complaining, what are you focusing on? All the sh** in your life. So guess what happens to you? You become a giant sh** magnet. Get the picture? I don't want to be around because they attract it to you. You got to get away from them. Because when you hear some complaining, it might hit you too, and it's the worst of all. That's what complaining does."

Jordan Belfort Summary

1. Take Action
2. Learn to Sell
3. Become Unconsciously Competent
4. Set Your Goals High
5. Have a Vision
6. Be Honest With Yourself
7. Get Rich Quick
8. Master Your Internal World
9. Try Your Hardest
10. Create Your Destiny

How can you apply these rules to your business or life today?

_____

_____

_____

_____

_____

_____

_____

_____

_____

_____

_____

_____

#DidYouKnow: Jordan Belfort's memoirs been published in 40 countries and translated into 18 languages.

"The best entrepreneurs do it because they want to make a change in the world and help people." – *Mark Zuckerberg*

- Computer programmer, entrepreneur, Facebook co-founder
- Launched Facebook from his Harvard dorm room in 2004
- In 2007, at the age of 23, he became a billionaire
- Consistently in the 100 most influential people in the world
- Receives a $1 salary as CEO of Facebook

Rule #1: You Get What You Spend Your Time Doing

"First of all, focus.

I think you basically get what you spend your time doing. I want the company to build three products this year, and we're going to work on a few others because people are interested in them, but those are the three things that I'm spending my product time on.

You get what you put into it.

If you spend a third of your time trying to make the people around you better through getting better people, mentoring, getting them to be better, getting the best people in your organization to ***more impactful roles*** then I think over time that's just accrues and you get a better organization."

Rule #2: Get Feedback

"We've had this tradition for seven or eight years at the company, where every week we have a ***Q&A where employees*** can come and ask me any question that they want about what's going on and what the direction of the company is or questions or things that they read about in the press or that their friends who use the product, what they're asking them.

And it's been this really important tradition for us. Both because we really believe in ***openness and communication*** and that's kind of what Facebook is all about, but it's also really important for me and for running the company to be able to get feedback, and to be able to learn what's on people's minds.

What our employees and folks who are a part of our team are thinking about, and a lot of the time, there are good questions that people ask that change the way that we think about what we're building and what we're here to do in the world, that often makes us go ***think and re-evaluate*** how we should be approaching different problems."

Rule #3: Make Mistakes

"So many things go wrong when you're starting a company, and often I think people ask, 'What mistakes should you avoid making?'

My answer to that is don't even bother trying to avoid mistakes because *you're going to make tons of mistakes.*

The important thing is actually learning quickly from whatever mistakes you make and *not giving up.*

There are things every single year of Facebook's existence that could have killed us, or made it so that it just seemed like moving forward and making a lot of progress just seemed intractable, but you just bounce back, and you learn, and nothing is impossible.

You just have to keep running through the walls."

Rule #4: Hire People You Would Work For

"I don't hire people who I wouldn't work for myself. I think that's a really good heuristic because everyone knows there's the saying: *'A players hire A players and B players hire C players',* which is good people hire good.

I don't think that that's that informative. It's not that useful.

I think a lot of the time the problem is you don't actually know. Sometimes you're trying to figure out how good someone is.

If you didn't think they were good, you wouldn't have hired them, but the heuristic of only hiring people who you would work for tends to be pretty good, I think, because then you know.

I would not work for this person then OK I'm not going to stretch just because I need to fill a role today."

Rule #5: Make a Change in the World [Evan's Fav]

"When you're starting something, it's just hard. You need to be pretty headstrong about it. There's going to be all these challenges that come up, and I think **the main thing that you need to do is just not give up.**

Know what you want to do and, the best entrepreneurs who I've met, don't really start companies because their goal is to build a company.

They do it because they **want to make a change in the world, and help people.**

And I think if you stay true to that and if you just focus on powering through no matter what the challenges are that will inevitably come up in your path, then you'll find that there are lots of **tools that are available** and a lot of **people who will help you** build what you're building."

Rule #6: Learn from the People Around You

"One definition that I have for a good team is a group of people that **makes better decisions as a whole than would individually make as a sum of the parts.**

I think most **smart people like learning.** That's one of the thrills of starting a company.

The learning curve can be so steep and if you can set up a team dynamic, where you're constantly learning from the people around you then what's better?

These are the people I wake every morning to. I want to go learn from and work from. And when building a team you want to think about the dynamics so that way you can maintain this property that **the team makes better decisions as a group than any individual would."**

Rule #7: Start Small

"We had a very simple focus and idea. The goal wasn't to make a huge community site. It was to make something where you could type in someone's name and find out a bunch of information about them. *So I took a few days and just threw together Facebook* and launched it on February 4th, 2004.

In the last tech bubble, most websites were run using these really expensive machines, which made it that you had to basically go and raise money before you could do anything. *We ran the site originally for $85 a month."*

Rule #8: Give the Very Best Experience

"Are we trying to optimize newsfeed to give each person, all of you guys, the best experience when you're reading or we're trying to help businesses to just reach as many people as possible? And in every decision that we make, *we optimize for the first.*

Making it so that when, for the people, who we serve, who use Facebook and are reading newsfeed *get the very best experience that they can.*

That means that if a business is sharing content that's going to be useful for them, then we'll show that. But that means that if the business is sharing content that isn't going to be useful for them, we may not show that because it's probably more important that they learn about their friends who had a baby and their baby is healthy.

That's an important guiding principle for how we think about this, and as the products continue to develop there's just going to be more people sharing more things and we're going to continue to try to do our best at showing the best thing that we can.

So if you're a business owner and you're thinking about how to use your free page on Facebook, I would just focus on trying to *publish really good content that's going to be compelling to your customers* and the people who are following you."

Rule #9: Care the Most About It

"I actually spend a bunch of time analyzing and reflecting on why it was that we were even able to do it because all reason suggests that we shouldn't have been able to do it.

Because all these other companies had way more engineering power, and servers, and time, and money, and all this stuff, and I actually think that this is a pretty instructive thing for anything that you want to go do because the same probably is going to be true for anything that you guys start. Someone else is going to have more resources. The reason why I think we actually ended up being the ones doing it is because *we just cared way more about it than everyone else.*

Early on there were all these skeptics saying that 'Oh, this can't be a business.' We didn't actually care that much about it being a business early on, but a lot of the reason why bigger companies didn't invest in it was because it wasn't clear that there was a model that would work for it. And I actually think that that's true for a lot of the best ideas. It's not that someone else can't do it, they actually can, and the odds are stacked against you, but I think often that *belief in the fact that you just care so much about what you're doing is the only thing that kind of drives you to do it* and, to be honest, that kind of drives me to this day.

I actually think a lot of the reason why great stuff gets built is because it's kind of irrational at the time, but it selects where the people who care the most about it doing it."

Rule #10: Social Bonds Are Critical

"The students around me were really important both in high school and in college. The people who started Facebook with me, a lot of people who are still with me, running the company today are people who I met when I was at Harvard. We had social bonds and academic bonds and I just I wouldn't understate the importance of that. It's very tied into my whole philosophy and the product that I spend my life building Facebook *because we just believe that social bonds are critical."*

Mark Zuckerberg Summary

1. You Get What You Spend Your
   Time Doing
2. Get Feedback
3. Make Mistakes
4. Hire People You Would Work For
5. Make a Change in the World
6. Learn from the People Around You
7. Start Small
8. Give the Very Best Experience
9. Care the Most About It
10. Social Bonds Are Critical

How can you apply these rules to your business or life today?

_____

_____

_____

_____

_____

_____

_____

_____

_____

_____

#DidYouKnow: Mark Zuckerberg has pledged to give away 99% of his wealth.

"We all go through doubt. It's hard. Those difficult moments are what build your character." – Joe Rogan

- Comedian, podcaster, and sports color commentator
- Began a career in stand-up in August 1988 in the Boston area
- Worked for the UFC as an interviewer and commentator
- His podcast is among the most popular in the world
- Is an advocate of physical and mental well-being

Rule #1: Be the Hero of Your Own Movie

"Be the hero of your own movie. If your life was a movie and it started now, what would the hero of your life's movie do? We define ourselves far too often by our past failures. We look at our past and we say, 'Well, that's me.' That's not you! You are this person right now. You're the person who's learned from those failures and you can choose to be the hero of your own movie right now. Write down your goals. Write down things you want to improve. *Write down things you won't tolerate from yourself.* Write down things that you've done in the past that you never want to see yourself do again and go forth from here as the hero of your own movie. Build momentum, build confidence and momentum with each good decision that you make from here on out. You can do it. Anyone can do it. We live in unique times. We live in one of the rarest times in human history where you can choose almost all of the input that comes your way. Whether it's the movies that you watch, the books you read, the podcasts you listen to, *you can choose to be inspired.* Do that. And be the hero of your own movie."

Rule #2: Be the Best Version of Yourself

"It's good to treat other people the way you would like to be treated yourself. It's a Golden Rule and there's a reason for it. And that reason is that we're connected in some strange way that we don't totally understand. And unless you are good to other people around you, unless you're kind and friendly and warm and loving, you're not going to enjoy this life. You're just not. They're going to be problems everywhere you go. You're going to have problems everywhere you go. We need to figure out like now, today, *what is the best way to live your life?* There's got to be ways you could be putting forth the most positive energy. What else do you want to do with your life? Don't be doing something you don't enjoy. Don't get locked into a car that you can't afford and doing something crazy because you need the money. Don't do that. *Do what you want to do.* Do what it is that you really want to do. Because if someone else is doing it, you can do it. Everybody makes their own path through this world but a lot of people don't follow the path that they really feel pulled to."

Rule #3: Stop Making Excuses *[Evan's Fav]*

"There's a bunch of people that will say, 'I have a family so it's a great idea for you to just go out there and go crazy.' I have people to support.' You need to listen. Stop saying that! Stop saying any of those things. Every single person who has ever done anything worthwhile or exceptional or difficult or extraordinary, anyone, whether it's great artists or authors or mathematicians, everyone encounters difficulties. *There is no easy road.* It does not exist. It is impossible. Everyone has issues. When you come up with excuses for why other people are successful and you're not, that is dangerous. When you give yourself an escape. 'Well, that's easy for you to say.' Everybody has a hard road. I wanted to jump out a window several times during my young life. I wanted to jump in front of a train. Just end it because it's just too much pressure. We all go through hard times. We all go through depression. We all go through doubt and moments in your life where it's really difficult and you're trying to figure what your path is going to be. It's hard. That is what makes you a person. And *those difficult moments are what build your character.* Show me a great man who's the son of a great man. These kids that are born billionaires, you're never going to be a self-made person. You have a backup trust for your trust."

Rule #4: Explore Difficult Tasks

"I'm fascinated by martial arts. I'm fascinated by comedy. I'm fascinated by many, many different things. *I don't understand when people say they're bored.* If I had the time to live 100 lives I'd be speaking different languages. I'd be living in different countries. I would try a number of different careers because I think there's a lot of unbelievable fascinating, puzzling, complex things that you could study in this world. I think that is one of the things that motivated me to explore difficult tasks because *through difficult tasks, you learn an incredible amount about yourself.* And you, through the fire of competition, you get to understand motivation. You get to understand the resistance that you have inside your mind to doing hard work. You get to understand the rewards of discipline. You don't truly appreciate relaxation unless you've worked hard and that is the yin and the yang of life. *One of the worst decisions a man can make is to be comfortable.*"

Rule #5: Push Forward

"There's a lot of folks that live life on a cushy cloud of marshmallows. And then one day something goes wrong and that's why spoiled kids are so sad. A spoiled young boy is one of the saddest things ever. A young boy that becomes a man and can't take care of himself and his dad has to keep on rescuing him.

His dad has to keep on bailing him out of situations and giving him money. I've met guys like that. And that is a crippling affliction when they don't have the character themselves to be able to get by in life. They constantly need someone to help them and bail them out. Even as a grown man, I've met guys in their 40s that still need help from their parents.

I'm like, 'Man, you're never going to get it right.' Because somewhere along the line they didn't face enough of the adversity to realize that there's sometimes you just got to get up and get done. That *sometimes we have to pull yourself up and you have to push forward even if you want to stay in bed.*

And if you don't and you're just calling on your daddy and your daddy keeps rescuing you, you never develop those tools. You never develop that ability to recognize what you're doing wrong with your life because you're soft. You got it cushiony. You got a safety net, a safety net for your safety net."

Rule #6: Work Towards Something

"If you had a 20 year old and he's just a doper where he wakes and bakes and doesn't get anything done. He's just always hanging out with his friends and playing video games and he's just a loser. I wish there was a way you could show someone like that: *Your life would feel better and richer if you had a goal, you chased that goal.* You would get this boost of confidence. You would get this boost of self-esteem.

Maybe you're into drawing comic books. Maybe you're into making pottery or sculptures. *Find whatever that is and pursue that instead of doing nothing."*

Rule #7: Have Discipline

"The one thing that discipline definitely helps you with is you get things done. And when you get things done, when you actually do things, you have more success. A big part of success is just not being f***ing lazy and just doing it. *90% of it is just showing up.* Get there. Start working. You're not going to feel perfect every day. If I only worked out when I felt good, I'd be a fat f*** because there's a lot of days I don't want to do it. Through discipline I get things done. I'm the most lazy, disciplined person I know because *I don't want to do it but I always do.*"

Rule #8: Don't Get Stuck in Life

"When you're alone with your thoughts, you get an idea of what your thoughts actually are. *If you live your life just acting constantly on the momentum of other people's expectations*, of you wanting to be liked by these other people, you can run into a trap and you set up a life that you didn't really want. You're trapped in this situation where you have a mortgage. You have credit card bills. You got student loans you have to pay. You have a bunch going on that you have to continue to feed, especially if you have a family. Then you're fully locked in. You can't take any chances and often times, people make the mistake of getting stuck and it is just a tactical mistake just like it would be a mistake if you got stuck in a video game. Just like it would be a mistake if you followed a map incorrectly and you got stuck in the woods.

Sometimes you have to back up and try again and if you're in a position where you can't back up and try again, you've trapped yourself. It's up to you to see that video game problem. To see that issue as it comes up on the map. To see all the problems that could potentially lay in front of you and calculate your future. And also look around at all the people that didn't do it and look at the misery that they're in and learn that you don't want to be like them. And then look at the people that have taken chances and navigated their way. What did they do differently than you? What objectivity do they have that maybe you lack? *The person who's able to look at themselves the closest is going to get the more rational results.*"

Rule #9: Spend Time in Nature

"One of the things that's **causing this funk** that people are in is that we're living our lives in these very unfulfilling ways where you're going to this office with artificial light and you're doing something you don't want to do all day long and then you get home and you're tired. And on top of that, you're eating potato chips and you're drinking soda and your body is just like, 'What is this?' **We're supposed to be out in the fields.** We're supposed to be walking up hills. We're supposed to be looking for animals or gathering vegetables. We're supposed to be doing all these things that our body's designed to do. **We're supposed to be in nature and nature is like a medicine.** It literally is a medicine to you. You don't have to go hunting. You don't have to go fishing. Just go hike man. Just go hike up to the top of a mountain and look out. There's a reward that you get that is intensely soul filling."

Rule #10: Pursue Your Desires

"**You should always be seeking to improve.** The connection with human beings on a very positive level where you build up a trust and you have warmth and friendship and you root for each other and you share in each other's bounty and you build together. We all know inherently in our heads that kindness is one of the best gifts you can bestow another human being. Whatever it is, we know that inherently that feels great. We know it. We have to figure out how to use our resources together so that we can be like that all the time. **I think it's always about doing what you actually want to be doing with your life.** There's a lot of people who just always wanted to be singers and they just, for whatever reason, never pursued it. So they just sing around their house and they always wonder what could've been if they just tried to be a singer. That's one form of a road block in your life. The depressed feeling that you didn't try. That you didn't try to reach your potential. You didn't go after what is intriguing to you. We all have almost like a beacon that pulls us in a certain direction. **The happiness that's involved in pursuing your inherent desires is unavoidable.** People think, 'Well all you have to do is find a career.' Yes, all you have to do is find a career. But I guarantee you there's one out there that you really, really want to do."

Joe Rogan Summary

1. Be the Hero of Your Own Movie
2. Be the Best Version of Yourself
3. Stop Making Excuses
4. Explore Difficult Tasks
5. Push Forward
6. Work Towards Something
7. Have Discipline
8. Don't Get Stuck in Life
9. Spend Time in Nature
10. Pursue Your Desires

How can you apply these rules to your business or life today?

_____

_____

_____

_____

_____

_____

_____

_____

_____

_____

_____

_____

#DidYouKnow: Joe Rogan is a Jiu-Jitsu black belt. He became interested in it after watching Royce Gracie at UFC 2: No Way Out.

"Be open to taking some risks and not being afraid to fail. Failure is the key to success." – Michelle Obama

- Lawyer, writer, and former First Lady of the United States
- Was the first African-American First Lady
- Graduate of Princeton University and Harvard Law School
- Served on the Board of the Chicago Council on Global Affairs
- Advocate for women, poverty awareness, and healthy eating

Rule #1: Keep Moving Forward *[Evan's Fav]*

"Some of you have been homeless. Some of you have risked the rejection of your families. Many of you have lain awake at night wondering how on earth you were going to support your parents and your kids. And many of you know what it's like to live not just month to month or day to day, but meal to meal. Let me tell you, you should never, ever, be embarrassed by those struggles. You should never view your challenges as a disadvantage. Instead, it's important for you to understand that **your experience facing and overcoming adversity is actually one of your biggest advantages.** Life will put many obstacles in your path. You'll have unreasonable bosses and difficult clients and patients. You'll experience illnesses and losses, crises and setbacks that will come out of nowhere and knock you off your feet. **Keep moving through the pain. Keep moving forward.**"

Rule #2: Be Authentic

"I've always felt a deep sense of obligation to make the biggest impact possible with this incredible platform, so I took on issues that were personal to me. Now, some folks criticize my choices for not being bold enough, but these were my choices, my issues, and I **decided to tackle them in a way that felt most authentic to me,** in a way that was both substantive and strategic, but also fun and hopefully inspiring, so I immersed myself.

I worked with Congress on legislation, gave speeches to CEO's, military generals, Hollywood executives, but I also worked to ensure that my efforts would resonate with kids and families. I planted a garden and hula-hooped on the White House lawn with kids. I did some mom dancing on TV. At the end of the day, **by staying true to the me I've always known,** I found that this journey has been incredibly freeing because no matter what happened, I had the peace of mind of knowing that all of the chatter, the name calling, the doubting, all of it was just noise. It did not define me. It didn't change who I was. And most importantly, it couldn't hold me back. I have learned that as long as I hold fast to my beliefs and values and follow my own moral compass, then **the only expectations I need to live up to are my own.**"

Rule #3: Work Hard

"Barack and I were both raised by families who didn't have much in the way of money or material possessions, but who had given us something far more valuable: Their *unconditional love.* Their unflinching sacrifice and the chance to go places they had never imagined for themselves. My father was a pump operator at the city water plant and he was diagnosed with multiple sclerosis when my brother and I were young and, even as a kid, I knew there were plenty of days when he was in pain and I knew there were plenty of mornings when it was a struggle for him to simply get out of bed. But every morning I watched my father wake up with a smile, grab his walker, prop himself up against the bathroom sink, and slowly shave and button his uniform, and when he returned home after a long day's work, my brother and I would stand at the top of the stairs of our little apartment patiently waiting to greet him, watching as he reached down to lift one leg and then the other to slowly climb his way into our arms.

But despite these challenges, my dad hardly ever missed a day of work. *He and my mom were determined to give me and my brother the kind of education they could only dream of."*

Rule #4: Don't Be Afraid to Fail

"You've got to be open to taking some risks and not being afraid to fail. *Failure is the key to success* so when you get to college, you got to raise your hand. You have to be engaged. Don't be the kid thinking, 'Well, I shouldn't be here and maybe I'm not smart enough and maybe, you know...' No! You are more than capable of being successful and going on, doing whatever you want in life. I sit here because I am you all. There is no difference between me and you. Working class kid growing up on the South Side of Chicago. Growing up with doubts and fears just like all of you all do. I know exactly how you all are feeling and kids out there who are thinking maybe I'm not ready. Maybe I'm not good enough. Maybe I can't afford it. But what teachers and mentors have told me is that, yes, you can and you must. *So get in there and be bold with your intelligence.* Raise your hand. Get support when you need it and know that we all got here because somebody helped us."

Rule #5: Choose Your Own Path

"I want you all to stay true to the most real, most sincere, most authentic parts of yourselves.

I want you to ask those basic questions: *Who do you want to be? What inspires you? How do you want to give back?*

And then I want you to take a deep breath and trust yourselves to chart your own course and make your mark on the world.

Maybe it feels like you're supposed to go to law school, but what you really want to do is teach little kids.

Maybe your parents are expecting you to come back home after you graduate, but you're feeling a pull to travel the world.

I want you to listen to those thoughts.

I want you to act with both your mind, but also your heart.

And no matter what path you choose, I want you to make sure it's you choosing it and not someone else."

Rule #6: Earn Success

"We learned about dignity and decency.

That *how hard you work matters more than how much you make.*

That helping others means more than just getting ahead yourself.

We learned about honesty and integrity. That the truth matters.

That you don't take shortcuts or play by your own set of rules.

And success doesn't count unless you earn it fair and square."

Rule #7: Take Your Role Seriously

"One of the things I know from sitting in this position is that every First Lady feels some level of pressure. I mean, this is a big platform and you don't want to mess it up.

So I wouldn't dare to compare my experience to any former First Lady, but I do **take the role seriously.**

I do, as I said in my convention speech, know that kids are watching us and watching what we say, what we do, and Barack and I have tried to make sure that what kids are seeing is something that they can be proud of because it matters."

Rule #8: Enjoy the Balance

"I have never been the kind of person who's **defined myself** by a career or a job. I just never have.

People used to ask me that during the course of the campaign, 'Is it hard for you to step off the track and devote your life to his dream?'

But the truth is that I believe in this man as our President and his vision for the country and if that meant stepping away from my particular job for a year and a half or for four or for eight years, if you do what you're supposed to do, then that's a small sacrifice to make.

I've got these great kids too. And the truth is I love kids and I love my kids and this isn't to say anyone who's working doesn't, but **I enjoy the balance of having a job and having a set of projects and being able to have times to make sure that I'm in the girls' lives** and making sure that we have time as a family.

That's a full plate. I don't view myself as being in a position where I'm twiddling my thumbs and wondering how am I going to get through the day.

I've **never experienced** that in my life."

Rule #9: Do What is Hard

"We are playing a long game here and that change is hard and change is slow and it never happens all at once, but eventually we get there. We always do.

We get there because of folks like my dad, folks like Barack's grandmother. Men and women who said to themselves, 'I may not have a chance to fulfill my dreams, but maybe my children will.' Maybe my grandchildren will.

See, so many of us stand here tonight because of their sacrifice and longing and steadfast love because time and again they *swallowed their fears and doubts and did what was hard."*

Rule #10: Empower Yourself

When you are struggling, and you start thinking about giving up, I want you to *remember the power of hope.*

The belief that something better is always possible if you're willing to work for it and fight for it.

It is our hope that if we work hard enough and believe in ourselves then we can be whatever we dream, *regardless of the limitations that others may place on us.*

The hope that when people see us for who we truly are, maybe just maybe, they too will be inspired to rise to their best possible selves. So don't be afraid. You hear me? Young people, don't be afraid. *Be focused. Be determined. Be hopeful. Be empowered.*

Empower yourselves with a good education, then get out there and use that education to build a country *worthy of your boundless promise.*

Lead by example with hope, never fear, and know that I will be with you, rooting for you and working to support you for the rest of my life."

Michelle Obama Summary

1. Keep Moving Forward
2. Be Authentic
3. Work Hard
4. Don't Be Afraid to Fail
5. Choose Your Own Path
6. Earn Success
7. Take Your Role Seriously
8. Enjoy The Balance
9. Do What is Hard
10. Empower Yourself

How can you apply these rules to your business or life today?

_____

_____

_____

_____

_____

_____

_____

_____

_____

_____

_____

_____

#DidYouKnow: Michelle Obama's high school teachers told her not to apply to Princeton, saying she was 'setting her sights too high.'

"That mountain can't be conquered. We conquered the limitations that are within ourselves." – Bob Proctor

- One of the living masters of The Law of Attraction
- Worked in the area of mind potential for more than 50 years
- Mentored under Earl Nightingale from 1968 to 1973
- Founder of Proctor Gallagher Institute.
- Featured in the blockbuster movie hit, The Secret

Rule #1: Discover Your Purpose

"I don't think you determine what your purpose is. *I think you discover what your purpose is.* There's a difference. Determining indicates deciding, and I don't think you decide. I think, if you go about it the right way, you discover it. There's some people that should be painting all day. They're great artists, like Michelangelo, who was obviously a great artist, a great sculptor. That was his purpose in his life. *Your purpose is why you get out of bed in the morning.* Do you know why you get up? If you're ever doing what everybody's doing, you're probably going in the wrong direction. Your purpose is your reason for living. What you want to do is sit down, and take a pen and a pad, and then ask yourself, *What do I really love doing?'* Now since you don't ask yourself that question every day, it might take a while for the answer to come to the surface. It comes to your consciousness and it may take a while. You may have to do this every morning for three months. But it would be well-invested, the time."

Rule #2: Don't Waste Your Minutes

"How many times have you had somebody say to you, 'Have you got a minute?' I want you to think about that. I read a poem one time, it said, 'I have only just a minute. Only 60 seconds and it was forced upon me. I can't refuse it. I didn't seek it and I didn't choose it. But it's up to me to use it. I must suffer if I lose it. Give account if I abuse it. *It's only a tiny little minute but eternity is in it.'* Do you know, if you're earning $50,000 a year, a minute's 42 cents? A half hour is $12.50. If you're earning $80,000 a year, a minute's 67 cents. Half hour is $20. If you're earning $150,000 a year, you got a minute? It costs you $1.25 a minute, and a half hour is $37.50. If somebody said, 'Do you want to stop for a cup of coffee?' Well, if you're earning a quarter of a million dollars a year, a minute is $2.08, half hour is $62.50. And then of course, you've got the coffee to pay for on top of that. The point is this: This is all we've got, right here, right now. We don't know how much we have left in the future, but we do know what we've got now, and I have found that people that win are the people who make up their mind. *They're not going to waste minutes. They're going to be productive. They're going to make it happen, every minute.*"

Rule #3: Be Different

"Success was the *progressive realization* of a worthy ideal. Anyone that has a goal, and they're moving towards it, they're successful. Most people think that you're successful if you have a lot of money. Quite often, you have a lot of money if you're successful, but I wouldn't say Mother Teresa has a lot of money, but she's a pretty successful lady.

I think there's two barriers. One is our conditioning. The conditioning that takes place in our *subconscious mind,* from the time we're infants. All we can do is act and talk like the people around us. That's why we learned the language we learned. We have a real strong conditioning, usually, with some not very good ideas. That's the barrier that's inside us. The one that's outside of us is our environment. We have a tendency to act like everybody around us, and if you think about this, it doesn't make a lot of sense, because 95% of the people live their entire life, and never live the way they want to live. Five percent of the people end up financially comfortable or independent. We all think different thoughts, and I believe *we should start to think, and build images in our mind,* of what we'd like to do, and then set out and do it."

Rule #4: Seek Failures

"You should seek failures. *If you're playing it safe, you're not going to win.* If you're playing it safe, like that old saying you were taught when you were little, 'Better to be safe than sorry.' Well that's a bunch of crap. It's not better to be safe than sorry. *It's by trying things that you figure out how far you can go.* You've got to get outside the box. Edison tried 1,000 ways before he built the incandescent light. He said, he didn't fail 1,000 times, he said there were 1,000 different steps to building a light bulb. Well there's different steps to get to where you're going. And I really do treat winning and losing exactly the same. I do not let it upset me.

I try anything. If I'm into an idea, the idea of losing never enters my mind. *If you're not prepared to lose, you're never going to win because you're always playing it safe.* There's no reward in that."

Rule #5: Conquer Your Own Limitations [*Evan's Fav*]

"Look at these two men. One was an ordinary beekeeper and the other, a Sherpa guide, from Nepal. Now there's Mt. Everest. Do you know, for thousands of years, people had tried to get to the top of Mt. Everest? People died doing it. It was believed it couldn't be done. They didn't know how to get to the top of the mountain, and that's what stops most people, because they don't know how. As little kids, we'd go, 'Mommy, Daddy, I want this,' and they'd say, *'Now how are you going to do that?'* Well, as a little kid, you don't know how to do it, but they did it. In 1953, on the 29th of May, they were the first two to get to the top of that mountain. They stood right at the top of the world. Do you know there's been over 1,000 people do it since then? I watched a young woman being interviewed, not very big, she'd just come back from going to the top of Mt. Everest. And the reporter asked her, 'How does it feel now that you've conquered the mountain?' She said, *'We didn't conquer the mountain. That mountain can't be conquered. We conquered the limitations that are within ourselves.'*"

Rule #6: Go to Experts for Advice

"Select a person who is already doing something that you'd like to do. *Get to know that person. Go to the experts for advice.* Don't ask the person next door, or your mother, father, or brother, or the guy that works beside you, because they don't necessarily know. There's no point in asking a person how to earn a lot of money if they're only earning $10,000 a year. They don't know. If they knew, they'd probably be earning a lot. *Don't go to a sick doctor if you want to get healthy.* You find someone that you can go to for advice. Get a real good book and lock into that book and start studying. I've had this one that looks like a Bible. But this is Napoleon Hill's book, 'Think and Grow Rich.' I've been reading this thing now for 23 years. I'll probably read it for another 23 years. Now I've read a lot of books. I've got probably 1,000 books sitting in my den at home in my library. But the one that I carry, I carry it everywhere I go, and I read it all the time, is 'Think and Grow Rich,' and I never stop reading it."

Rule #7: Don't Worry About What Others Think of You

"You know, many years ago, I read a book by Terry Cole-Whittaker. It was a classic, *'What You Think of Me is None of My Business.'* Think of the amount of time that is wasted on negative energy, wondering what other people think of you. What they think of you really doesn't make any difference. It's what you think of you that makes a difference. So, as you go through the day, don't worry about what other people think of you. Just say, *'I'm alright. I'm God's highest form of creation.'*"

Rule #8: Crash Through the Terror Barrier

"On the other side of the terror barrier is something we call freedom. And you know, very few people get through that terror barrier. It's rather sad. Freedom is available to everyone. There isn't anyone that cannot live the way they want to live. Why don't they? They don't know. And they don't even know they don't know. *Fear causes them to stay where they are.* On a conscious level, we experience doubt. The doubt turns into an emotion called fear, and that fear is expressed through the body as anxiety. See, that person is getting emotionally involved to move ahead. Do you know what happens? They hit that terror barrier and they bounce off it, and right back into bondage, and they're so relieved to get back there. *They're back where they're comfortable.* They've canceled the sale. They've decided not to move. They're going to stay in the job that they don't like. At least they're comfortable.

Now, that's not a very good way to live, and do you know something? That's something everybody experiences if they're going to grow. You're going to hit that terror barrier. See, the terror barrier is going beyond where you're at, going to a new level. I'm going to tell you something: *When I set a goal, if it doesn't scare and excite me at the same time, I know I'm going in the wrong direction.* If you don't learn to go through the terror barrier, you're going to stay right where you are for the rest of your days. That's not a good place to be. What did Joseph Campbell say? So true. 'The cave you fear to enter holds the treasure you seek.'"

Rule #9: Develop Your Imagination

"The imagination is the most marvelous, miraculous, powerful force that the world has ever known. The average individual uses the imagination, if they use it at all, against themselves. They imagine what they don't want, problems coming. Do you know you can use your imagination to go into the future and bring it into the present? That's what all highly-successful people do. *They see where they want to go and then they act like the person they want to become.* It's the actor's technique. Act like the person you want to become. How do you do that? You use your imagination. It's inconceivable that people would wander around with so much power and potential, and squander it. The average person tip-toes through life, hoping they make it safely to death. It's such a shame and it doesn't have to be that way. The average individual really does not believe that they're creative. Everyone's creative. It's just that some have chosen to *use their creative faculties to a greater degree than others.* What do you want? How do you really want to live? Build the picture in your mind."

Rule #10: Change the Paradigm

"The law of attraction is always working. It's the thoughts that you're thinking, that you impress upon your subconscious mind that control the vibration the body's in, and *that dictates how you act,* but it also dictates what you attract. You attract energy that's in harmony with you. You attract people that are in harmony with you. You see, everything operates on frequencies. There's an infinite number of frequencies, but you and I operate on a frequency, just like a radio station does. And the only music you can attract is the music that is tuned in to the vibration you're in. Now it's the paradigm that has been controlling the vibration. *You can change your thinking,* but that doesn't do anything. You've got to change the paradigm. And if you don't change the paradigm, nothing happens. If you keep attracting what you don't want, understand this: It's the paradigm that's causing the problem. When we don't feel good, we're in a negative vibration. You want to feel good? Move into a positive vibration. Stop and think of what you're grateful for. *You will never attract wealth, happiness, health, until you get the paradigm to get you on that frequency.*"

Bob Proctor Summary

1. Discover Your Purpose
2. Don't Waste Your Minutes
3. Be Different
4. Seek Failures
5. Conquer Your Own Limitations
6. Go to Experts for Advice
7. Don't Worry About What Others Think of You
8. Crash Through the Terror Barrier
9. Develop Your Imagination
10. Change the Paradigm

How can you apply these rules to your business or life today?

_____

_____

_____

_____

_____

_____

_____

_____

_____

_____

#DidYouKnow: Bob Proctor has listened to the audio version of 'Think and Grow Rich' thousands of times.

"Work hard to get it. When you get it, reach back, pull someone else up. Aspire to make a difference." – Denzel Washington

- Actor, filmmaker, and philanthropist
- Won 3 Golden Globe awards and 2 Academy Awards
- Received the Cecil B. DeMille Lifetime Achievement Award
- Has donated millions to religious causes and the arts
- National spokesperson for Boys & Girls Clubs of America

Rule #1: Dreams Need Goals

"Dreams without goals are just dreams.

And they ultimately fuel disappointment.

Goals on the *road to achievement* cannot be achieved without discipline and consistency.

I pray that you all put your shoes way under the bed at night so that you've got to get on your knees in the morning to find them."

Rule #2: Bring Your Dreams to Life

"To get something you never had, you have to do something you never did.

Les Brown is a motivational speaker.

He made an analogy about this.

He says, 'Imagine you're on your deathbed, and standing around your deathbed are the *ghosts representing your unfulfilled potential.*

The ghost of the ideas you never acted on, the ghost of the talents you didn't use, and they're standing around your bed angry, disappointed, and upset.'

They say, 'We came to you because you could have brought us to life.

And now we have to go to the grave together.'

So I ask you today, how many ghosts are going to be around your bed when your time comes?"

Rule #3: Ignore the Opinions of Others

Interviewer: "You don't pay a lot of attention to reviews and those kind of things?"

Denzel Washington: "You're always affected by opinion, but the more opinions there are of me, the less I look at them, because I just can't live my life based upon what other people think about me. *So I can't concern myself too much with what other people think. It's just not healthy.* I don't think I could continue to do what I do if I was constantly worrying about what somebody thought about it."

Rule #4: Stick to Your Guns

"You don't have to compromise yourself. If it's something you don't feel good about, then don't do it. The most important choices I've made was to say no. And I've said no many a time to films, especially early on that I just didn't feel comfortable with.

There was one script that was brought to me, I called it 'the nigger they couldn't kill' because he was accused of raping his wife in the '40s, and they tried to hang him but he didn't die. And they tried to electrocute him, and they were like, 'It's a comedy!' I'm like, 'It isn't funny to me!'

So, I actually called Sidney Poitier, who I was fortunate at that time, and still, to be able to call. And I said, 'This movie's making me sick. And they offered me $600,000.'

He said to me, 'The first two, or three, or four films you make in this industry, Denzel, will determine how people see you.' I turned it down. I turned the money down. I needed the money. I turned it down. Six months later I got 'Cry of Freedom.'

So, stick to your guns. *If you don't feel like you should do it, then don't do it.* I think the most important decisions you could make is saying no."

Rule #5: Aspire to Make a Difference

"Anything you want, good.

You can have. So claim it.

Work hard to get it.

When you get it, reach back, pull someone else up.

Each one, teach one.

Don't just aspire to make a living.

Aspire to make a difference."

Rule #6: Share Your Gift

"You'll never see a U-Haul behind a hearse. I'll say it again. You'll never see a U-Haul behind a hearse.

Now I've been blessed to make hundreds of millions of dollars in my life.

I can't take it with me. And neither can you.

So it's not how much you have, it's what you do with what you have.

And we all have different gifts.

Some money, some love, some patience, some their ability to touch people, but we all have it.

Use it. Share it.

That's what counts.

Not what you're driving. Not what you're flying in. Not what kind of house you bought your mama."

Rule #7: Work Hard

"The one thing I'm the most happy about, in terms of my career, is the fact that *I got there just by working hard.*

Not partying with the right people. Not compromising myself in any way or cutting any kind of deals.

Just by working hard, just by plugging along, *sawing wood as I like to call it.* I'm a 20 year old sensation."

Rule #8: Fall Forward *[Evan's Fav]*

"I've found that nothing in life is worthwhile unless you take risks. Nothing. Nelson Mandela said, *'There is no passion to be found playing small and settling for a life that's less than the one you're capable of living.'*

Now I'm sure in your experiences in school and applying to college, and picking your major, and deciding what you want to do with life, I'm sure people have told you to make sure you have something to fall back on.

'Make sure you got something to fall back on, honey.'

But I never understood that concept, having something to fall back on. If I'm going to fall, I don't want to fall back on anything except my faith. I want to fall forward. I figure at least this way I'll see what I'm going to hit. Fall forward. This is what I mean.

Reggie Jackson struck out 2,600 times in his career, the most in the history of baseball. But you don't hear about the strikeouts.

People remember the home runs. Fall forward.

Thomas Edison conducted 1,000 failed experiments, did you know that? I didn't know that. Because the 1,001st was the light bulb.

Fall forward. Every failed experiment is one step closer to success."

Rule #9: Know Your Priorities

"I'm a father first. I don't get life mixed up with making a living. I was there for all four of my children being born. When the first one was born, I recognized the difference between life and making a living. They're life, you know? *Our family is life.* Acting is making a living."

Rule #10: Don't Quit

"You will fail at some point in your life, accept it. You will lose. You will embarrass yourself. You will suck at something. There's no doubt about it. *Embrace it,* because it's inevitable.

And I should know. In the acting business, you fail all the time. Early on in my career, I auditioned for a part in a Broadway musical. Perfect role for me, I thought. Except for the fact that I can't sing. So I'm about to go on stage, but they guy in front of me, he's singing like Pavarotti. He's just going on and on and on, and I'm just shrinking. I'm getting smaller and smaller. So, I come out with my little sheet music and it was 'Just My Imagination' by the Temptations. That's what I came up with. I hand it to the accompanist and she looks at it, and looks at me, and looks out at the director and is like, 'Alright.'

I didn't get the job. But here's the thing, I didn't quit. I didn't fall back. I walked out of there to prepare for the next audition, and the next audition, and the next audition. I prayed. I prayed, and I prayed. But I continued to fail, and fail, and fail. But it didn't matter, because you know what? There's an old saying, *'You hang around the barber shop long enough, sooner or later you're going to get a haircut.'* So you will catch a break, and I did catch a break.

Last year, I did a play called 'Fences on Broadway.' Won the Tony award. And I didn't have to sing, by the way. But here's the kicker, it was at the Court Theater. It was at the same theater that I failed that first audition 30 years prior. The point is every graduate here today has the training and the talent to succeed. *But do you have the guts to fail?"*

175

Denzel Washington Summary

1. Dreams Need Goals
2. Bring Your Dreams to Life
3. Ignore the Opinions of Others
4. Stick to Your Guns
5. Aspire to Make a Difference
6. Share Your Gift
7. Work Hard
8. Fall Forward
9. Know Your Priorities
10. Don't Quit

How can you apply these rules to your business or life today?

_____

_____

_____

_____

_____

_____

_____

_____

_____

_____

_____

_____

_____

#DidYouKnow: Denzel Washington is a devout Christian and has considered becoming a preacher.

"There's no room for excuses. Excuses are tools of the incompetent used to build bridges to nowhere." – Barack Obama

- 44th President of the United States
- 1st African American to hold the office of the President
- Graduate of Columbia University and Harvard Law
- Left office in January 2017 with a 60% approval rating
- Known for his Patient Protection and Affordable Care Act

Rule #1: Move the Ball Forward

"We looked at a whole slew of problems when we came into office.

And we said, 'Where can we advance the ball down the field each and every time, across the board?'

And we don't score a touchdown every time, but we move the ball forward.

You're always going to fall short because if you're hitting your marks that means you didn't set them high enough."

Rule #2: Have Hope

"Hope is imagining, and then fighting for, and then working for what did not seem possible before.

That's leadership.

John F. Kennedy didn't look up at the moon and say, 'Aww, that's too far.

We can't go. False hopes.'

Martin Luther King didn't stand on the steps of the Lincoln Memorial and say, 'Go home everybody.

The dream's deferred.

 False hopes.'

Ya'll need a reality check.

There is a moment in the life of every generation when that *spirit of hopefulness has to come through,* if we are to make our mark on history."

Rule #3: Don't Get Complacent

"We too often let the external, the **material things serve as indicators that we're doing well,** even though something inside us tells us that we're not doing our best.

That we're avoiding that which is hard, but also necessary, that we're shrinking from rather than rising to the challenges of the age. And the thing is, in this new hyper-competitive age, none of us, **none of us can afford to be complacent.**

That's true whatever profession you choose. Professors might earn the distinction of tenure but that doesn't guarantee that they'll **keep putting in the long hours and late nights** and have the passion and the drive to be great educators.

The same principle is true in your personal life. Being a parent is not just a matter of paying the bills, doing the bare minimum. It's not just bringing a child into the world that matters, but **the acts of love and sacrifice** it takes to raise and educate that child, and give them opportunity."

Rule #4: Stay Focused

"The one thing that I feel deeply about, and this is something I'll feel deeply about when I leave government is, **stuff gets better if we work at it and we stay focused on where we're going.** It doesn't immediately get solved and I warned against this when I was running for office, because everybody had the hope posters. This is going to be an ongoing project. And it's a project of citizens. It's not just, fix it. It's how do we work together to get things done, and it will be imperfect.

The VA is better now than when I came into office. Government works better than when I came into office. The economy, by every metric, is better than when I came into office. And so, the reason I can sleep at night, is I say to myself, 'You know what? It's better.' Now, am I satisfied with it? No, and should voters be satisfied with it? Absolutely not, because otherwise **if we get complacent and lazy then stuff doesn't happen.**"

Rule #5: You Can't Do it Alone

"You just don't succeed in any endeavor unless you've got a team that's been supporting you. And, that's part of my political philosophy. It's really based on my own experience, which was if somebody hadn't been out there looking out for me, starting with my mom, my grandmother, my grandfather, then I wouldn't have made it.

It wasn't because of my brilliance or something that these things happened, it had to do with *people investing in you.* And so we've got to make sure we're investing in the next generation, just like somebody invested in us."

Rule #6: Commit to Something Bigger

"I want to highlight two main problems with that old, tired 'me-first' approach to life. First of all, it distracts you from what's truly important. And it may *lead you to compromise your values and your principles and your commitments.* Think about it. It's in chasing titles and status and worrying about the next election rather than the national interests and the interests of those who you're supposed to represent, that politicians so often lose their ways in Washington.

They spend time thinking about polls, but not about about principle. It was in pursuit of gaudy short-term profits and the bonuses that came with them, that so many folks lost their way on Wall Street, engaging in extraordinary risks with other people's money. In contrast, the leaders we revere, the businesses and institutions that last, they are not generally the result of a narrow pursuit of popularity or personal advancement but of *devotion to some bigger purpose.*

The preservation of the Union, or the determination to lift a country out of a depression. *The creation of a quality product.* A commitment to your customers, your workers, your shareholders, and your community.

That's the hallmark of real success."

Rule #7: Stop Making Excuses

"We know that too many young men in our community continue to make bad choices. And I have to say growing up, I made quite a few myself. Sometimes I wrote off my own failings as just another example of the world trying to keep a Black man down. I had a tendency sometimes to make excuses for me not doing the right thing. But one of the things that all of you have learned over the last four years is *there's no longer any room for excuses.*

I understand there's a common Fraternity creed at Morehouse, *'Excuses are tools of the incompetent used to build bridges to nowhere and monuments of nothingness.'*

Well, we've got no time for excuses. Not because the bitter legacy of slavery and segregation have vanished entirely, they have not. Not because racism and discrimination no longer exist, we know those are still out there. It's just that in today's hyper-connected, hyper-competitive world with millions of young people from China and India and Brazil, many of whom started with a whole lot less than all of you did, all of them entering the global workforce alongside you.

Nobody is going to give you anything that you have not earned. Nobody cares how tough your upbringing was. Nobody cares if you suffered some discrimination. And moreover, you have to remember that whatever you've gone through, it pales in comparison to the hardships previous generations endured and they overcame them. And if they overcame them, *you can overcome them too.*"

Rule #8: Don't Take Yourself Too Seriously

"Part of the way that you survive the stress of the White House is being able to laugh with your team about some of the crazy stuff that happens. You can't take yourself too seriously. You have to take the job seriously. You have to take your responsibilities seriously. But, *you have to be able to laugh at yourself first* and foremost in order to be able to manage the whole thing."

Rule #9: Stick to Your Plan

"You have to have a plan. You have to have a strategy and then you have to have stick-to-it-ness because you know the strategy is not going to immediately bear fruit. The American character is one that lurches between spasm and trance. We get real exercise for about two weeks and then we fall asleep for two years. Our vision extends decades. It extends generations.

If we set the trend lines just a little bit better then the infant that's crying in Compton or Harlem, or Anacostia, or the Ninth Ward, that infant may have a different future. And then when that infant has a different future, the country has a different future. And then we as a people have a different future. So, there's got to be an understanding of *how time can actually help us move mountains.* If we're working with time, we're not waiting for time, we're working with it."

Rule #10: Follow Your Passion *[Evan's Fav]*

"You may have setbacks and you may have failures but you're not done. You're not even getting started. Not by a long shot. And if you ever forget that, just look to history. Thomas Paine was a failed corset maker, a failed teacher, and a failed tax collector before he made his mark on history with a little book called, 'Common Sense' that helped ignite a revolution.

Julia Child didn't publish her first cookbook until she was almost 50. Colonel Sanders didn't open up his first Kentucky Fried Chicken until he was in his 60's.

Winston Churchill was dismissed as little more than a has-been who enjoyed scotch a little bit too much before he took over as Prime Minister and saw Great Britain through it's finest hour.

Your body of work is never done. Each of them at one point in their life didn't have any title, or much status to speak of. But they had passion. A commitment to following that passion wherever it would lead and to working hard every step along the way."

Barack Obama Summary

1. Move the Ball Forward
2. Have Hope
3. Don't Get Complacent
4. Stay Focused
5. You Can't Do it Alone
6. Commit to Something Bigger
7. Stop Making Excuses
8. Don't Take Yourself Too Seriously
9. Stick to Your Plan
10. Follow Your Passion

How can you apply these rules to your business or life today?

_____

_____

_____

_____

_____

_____

_____

_____

_____

_____

_____

#DidYouKnow: Barack Obama loves playing basketball, often had pick-up games at the White House, and is left-handed.

"The people who wait end up getting cooked. The rule is simple. You do it now. You do it now." – Zig Ziglar

- Author, salesman, and motivational speaker
- First book, 'See You at the Top', got rejected by 30 publishers
- It has sold over 250,000 copies to date
- 8 of his 10 books reached bestseller lists
- Received the National Speakers Association Cavett Award

Rule #1: Have a Dream

"When you're asleep, ladies and gentlemen, you need your dreams. I'm here to tell you that when **you're wide awake you also need your dreams.** You must have your goals. You'll never make it as a wandering generality. You must become a meaningful specific. If you're going to work tomorrow because that's what you did yesterday you're not going to be as good tomorrow as you were yesterday because now you're two days older and no closer to the goal which you do not have. You can't make it as a wandering generality."

Rule #2: Think Like a Champion

"I sold heavy duty waterless cookware on the door-to-door demonstration plan. And, that was a marvelous experience. The first two and a half years I struggled financially. Now, that doesn't mean I didn't sell a lot, because I did. I sold my furniture. Sold my car. Then I went to a meeting and a man named P.C. Merrill persuaded me that I could be the number one salesman in America out of the 7,000 member sales force. He said, 'You've got everything that it takes to be a great salesman if you just believed in yourself and went to work on a regular schedule.'

I'd never had anybody say something like that to me. **'You could be a great one.** You could be the national champion.' Now, I've always been loved, but nobody ever thought of me as a champion. Because of Mr. Merrill's integrity and because he had written the training program and because he had set all of the records I took him absolutely at his word. The previous year I had not been in the top 5,000 out of that 7,000 member sales force. But the year after Mister Merrill got through with me I was number two out of the 7,000 and received the best promotion that was available in the company at that time. And, the interesting thing about the success that year, he did not really teach me that much about sales. I'd been in it two and half years at that point, but what he did teach me was about who I was. The picture I had of myself changed dramatically. **I started thinking as a champion and performing as a champion.** And, I did finish number two and had that wonderful promotion."

Rule #3: Be Committed

"Commitment plays heavily in everything. If you've made a commitment when you hit the rough spots, not if, when you hit the rough spots your immediate thought is, 'How can I solve the problem?'

If you have not made the commitment when you hit the rough spot whether it's in marriage or education or career or whatever your first thought is, 'Man, how can I get out of this deal?' And so, that commitment plays a huge role.

And, some people are about as committed as a kamikaze pilot on its 39th mission. I mean, they don't really take it that seriously."

Rule #4: Do it Right Now! *[Evan's Fav]*

"You ever have anybody say, 'Well, wait till the kids get out of school and then I'll really get involved in this project. We got so many things going on right now. Wait until they're out of school. Wait until the summer time comes then I'll really get busy.'

The kids get out of school, you know what they say then? 'Well, I didn't realize it but I've got to take the kids somewhere every day. I had more time when they were in school. Wait until they get back in school and then I'll really get busy.'

The people who wait for Aunt Matilda to move out or John to get onto the day shift or the new models to come out or the new mayor to come in or for the new advertising campaign to get started the people who wait on the new senator in Washington or until inflation slows or the rate of interest come down...

The people who wait for changes to take place out there before they do the changing in here are flat going to end up getting cooked.

The rule is simple. *You do it now. You do it now."*

Rule #5: Be Prepared

"How many of you feel like I've made this talk before? Several hundred times. I made it yesterday. You know what I did between yesterday and today? *I spent over six hours getting ready for today.* You see, I think it would be arrogant if I thought I could stand up and spit it out just because I did it yesterday or hundreds of times. That's arrogance. That's when Buster Douglas knocks out Mike Tyson. That's when an expansion team in Houston beats an established NFL team in Dallas. I dare not. Look at the people here, several thousand. I'm taking over an hour. That's several thousand hours of time. Where would my integrity be if I came here unprepared to make something, a presentation that could make a difference in your life. There is no way. **You've got to prepare for it** ladies and gentlemen."

Rule #6: Keep Your Word

"I almost did not go to the most important sales meeting. That morning I awakened. Five o'clock the alarm clock goes off, and it was an *alarm clock* in those days, now it's an *opportunity clock.* If I can hear that, it means I've got an opportunity to get up and go. When the clock went off I looked out and I said no sane person would ever get in a little automobile without a heater in weather like this and drive all the way to Charlotte to go to another meeting. So, I lay back down. As I lay down the words of my mother came back to me, 'Son, if you work for a man you work for him all the way. You're loyal to him in every way. And, *if your word is no good, you're no good.*'

I had promised this company, which had taken me two months to get the job, that if they would give me the opportunity I'd be at every sales meeting. I'd be at every training session. And, in two and a half years, despite my lack of success, I had been at every sales meeting, at every training session and I'd never even been late. The words of my mother came back. I rolled out of bed, went to the meeting. That's the one that changed my life. It changed my life because that's the day that Mr. Merrill persuaded me that I could be the champion. *It made all the difference in the world."*

Rule #7: Set Goals

"For 24 years of my adult life, by choice, I weighed well over 200 pounds. I say by choice because, you see, I have never accidentally eaten anything. It's always been deliberate. And, when I choose to eat too much today I have chosen to weigh too much tomorrow. *You can choose to set goals and realize your potential or you can choose not to set them.* Now, if you choose not to set them you've got to understand that the consequences are not going to be good down the road. For 24 years I was going to lose that weight. But, it wasn't until I wrote it down, put a date on it, listed the obstacles I had to overcome, identified the people, the groups, the organizations I needed to work with, spelled out a plan of action, set that time limit in there, and identified all of the benefits to me. It was only when I did that that the goal became a reality and I lost the weight.

For 10 or 15 years I was going to write a book. You know anybody who's going to do just a whole lot of things? I was going to write a book. But, it wasn't until I got busy writing the book and writing the plans first before the book ever materialized. The immortal J.C. Penny, many, many years ago said, *'Give me a stock clerk with a goal and I'll give you a man who'll make history. But give me a man without a goal and I'll give you a stock clerk.'* Yes indeed, ladies and gentlemen, you absolutely must have those goals."

Rule #8: Evaluate Where You Are

"What do you call success? Go down the list. And all I want you to do... go down the list, write whether you get a plus on that one or a minus on that one. You'll be the only one to see it, but it might be an eye opener. You see, *most people never dare to evaluate really where they are.*

And, you've got to know where you are before you can really determine your chances of getting what you really want out of life. That's what we need to do. Evaluate where we are. *Are we investing our time properly, using our resources properly? What will the end results be?"*

Rule #9: Have Integrity

"On the radio interviews I did, at least 90% of the first 25 of them would always start with the same thing. 'Zig, they tell me you could sell anything to anybody.' And I said, 'Yeah, they lied to you when they said that because you've just described a con artist.' No legitimate professional sales person would ever dream of selling anything that he did not fervently believe was in the best interest of the person he was selling to. Of all of the qualities a good sales person must have, **number one is integrity.** See, we are trained as sales people to persuade other people to buy, to make decisions. And, an unethical sales person can persuade people to buy things that they don't need, are overpriced, or they pressure them into buying it. A legitimate, integrity driven sales person **will only sell a product that will enable him to sell them again and again and again.** A product he would sell to his mother. That's the kind of sales person who has long term, balanced success."

Rule #10: The Reward Follows the Effort

"Unfortunately a lot of people are standing in front of the stove of life and they say, 'Now stove, you give me some heat then I'll put some wood in you.' That ain't the way it works. **You've got to put something in before you can get anything out.** So, many times you know the employee goes to the employer and says, 'Give me a raise and then I start coming to work on time.' Or, so many times they will come to them and say, 'Make me the boss. Now, I know I haven't been here very long, don't really deserve to be the boss but I function better when I am in charge of things. You reward me now, then I promise you I'll learn what this business is all about later on. Reward me now and I'll produce later.' Doesn't work that way. You've got to put something in before you can expect to get anything out. Isn't it true that anything worth doing is worth doing poorly until you can learn to do it well? We'll never know how many kids have missed a college scholarship because they didn't study an average of 10 more minutes a day. This is the story of success. This is the story of life. *I believe with all of my heart that if you will pump long enough and hard enough and enthusiastically enough that eventually the reward is going to follow the effort.*"

Zig Ziglar Summary

1. Have a Dream
2. Think Like a Champion
3. Be Committed
4. Do it Right Now!
5. Be Prepared
6. Keep Your Word
7. Set Goals
8. Evaluate Where You Are
9. Have Integrity
10. The Reward Follows the Effort

How can you apply these rules to your business or life today?

_____

_____

_____

_____

_____

_____

_____

_____

_____

_____

_____

_____

#DidYouKnow: Zig Ziglar's first book was rejected by 30 publishers and went on to sell over 250,000 copies.

"Anger really destroys the part of your brain which can judge right or wrong." – Dalai Lama

- 14th and current Dalai Lama, Tenzin Gyatso
- Received the Nobel Peace Prize in 1989
- Keeps a busy lecture and teaching schedule in his 80's
- Tied Barack Obama as the most popular world leader in 2013
- 1 of only 6 people ever given Honorary Canadian Citizenship

Rule #1: Help Others

"The ultimate source of satisfaction is within ourselves.

If you do wrong, things mainly harming others, you get negative consequences.

If you are helping others, it brings more happiness to others, you get benefit.

More inner strength and more confidence of purpose of life and fulfillment about that purpose.

Then you always feel happy."

Rule #2: Don't Care What Others Say [Evan's Fav]

"Some say good person, some say bad person.

It doesn't matter so long as my own motivation for thinking is honest, sincere.

That's important.

That's simple Buddhist monk.

Actually, Buddha as he taught, *'Don't care what others say.'*

If one says too much praise, then at that time should think, 'Oh, I also have the critics.'

Then, one says a lot criticism, then you should think, 'Oh, some people are praising me.'

So, it doesn't matter.

Too much paying attention to these things are silly."

Rule #3: Pay Attention to Your Inner Values

"The ultimate source of a happy life is our inner value. Irrespective of a believer or nonbeliever, whether it be religion or not. We should pay more attention to our inner world.

Now according to the latest of scientific findings, it is now clear, even with good health or a healthy body, **the healthy mind is very essential.**

A more peaceful mind brings a healthy body because the mind is calm, peaceful. Then our body elements also remain more balanced.

So that brings a healthy body. Too much stress, too much worry, disturbs our body element. That creates certain sort of problems in the body. So therefore, *a calm mind is very essential."*

Rule #4: Be Calm

"I think you should realize that anger may bring some kind of energy for a short period. But that energy is actually blind energy. And **anger really destroys the part of your brain which can judge right or wrong.** So when we fully develop anger, we can't see the reality.

So that energy is more bold, right? But that energy is blind energy. So in order to face the problem, our method should be realistic. In order to carry a realistic method, you must know the reality. When we look at the reality, when we investigate the reality, **our mind should be calm.**

Otherwise we cannot see the thing objectively.

So in order to use human intelligence properly, our mind should be calm. So taking this line, anger firstly destroys your inner peace. Secondly, it destroys your ability to investigate the reality.

So if you think this way, then once you have clear evidence, anger is of no use, only destruction."

Rule #5: Have Compassion

"Affection, or compassionate attitude, warm-heartedness, is very, very important for one's own wellbeing, for one's own happiness. So don't consider the practice of compassion is something of a religious matter, or practice of compassion is something good for others, not necessarily to oneself. That is totally a mistake. Since childhood, we are already equipped with this seed of compassion. Now that seed, you must keep, nurture all your life. Then using reasons, evidence, that seed of compassion can further develop unbiased compassion. Not depending on other's attitude but rather other's being itself. So that kind of compassion can reach your enemy. So that compassion is infinite compassion, unbiased compassion, real compassion. *So if we become a compassionate person, then your life becomes meaningful.* Because you yourself are happy, calm, peaceful. Then your friends, including animals, also should get peace. So at the last day of your life you feel happy. All my life, I'll spend peaceful, friendly. You really feel happy. Otherwise, at that moment, even if you're a billionaire, ghost money, nothing can be used. If your whole life is a more compassionate life, then you feel no regret. So a purposeful life is a naturally happy life, meaningful life."

Rule #6: Be Determined

"Another important factor is *determination*. You should not think these developments can take place within a few days or few years. You see that these developments even may take eons. So you see our determination doesn't matter even may take millions of billions of billions of eons. It doesn't matter. If you're really wasting a life, the purpose of a life, then even one day is too long. So once you're determined, once you make up your mind, some kind of firm determination, and clear objective way, then time is not important. So long as space remains, so long as sentient beings suffering remain, I will remain in order to serve. You see that sentence really gives me some kind of understanding, and also I think it's inspiring. *I think we must receive practice step by step with patience, with determination.* Once you involve, are dedicated, or determined to practice, then some improvement you can see. To change, not easy, not easy."

Rule #7: Meditate

"When we feel a sense of irritation, during that moment, if that person concentrates fully on the breathing, nothing else, breathing, *one, two, three, five, 10, 15, 20.*

When your mental state is irritated, but then after 20, 30, short breathing, your mental state will be a little different, *a little more calm.*

Since we are dealing with *emotions*, the best method to deal with that is through *meditation.*

Not for the next life, not for Heaven, but for your day to day well-being."

Rule #8: Find Life's Meaning

"I think the best method to avoid fear or regret at the time of death is *while we are alive, our time, our energy must be utilized in a meaningful way.*

That's the most profound meaning of usefulness.

One's own survival, even animals, also do this.

But service to others, is something unique about human beings.

So, *serving other people, helping other people* is, I think is a very, very appropriate sort of action according to human ability.

We have such ability to utilize that ability.

The most appropriate way is serving other people. Then, at the end, *you feel no regret.*

I've done my best to live some sort of meaningful life. Now when the end comes, although sorry, sad, but no regrets."

Rule #9: Develop Friendships

"We are social animals. And particularly, in modern time, the reality, economy, environment, and many things are heavily interdependent. That is reality. So even from this selfish viewpoint you have to **take care about others' well-being.** You just think of yourself, blind selfish, think for yourself, forget others. Or worse things. Exploit others, cheating others, bullying others, ultimately you suffer. Through these mischievous ways you may gain some temporary sort of benefit but deep inside you feel uncomfortable.

Then eventually, you truly become a lonely person. Nobody loves you. Nobody respects you. If you take care of others, as a human brother or sister, sincerely, seriously, then everybody becomes your friend. So when you have a truly trusted friend there, if you need something, you can ask them. If you become friendless or a lonely person, when you are really facing some problems, nobody will share. **We are social animals.**"

Rule #10: Conquer Yourself

"What's important isn't that different emotions are right. This is the ultimate enemy, or the source of suffering. So all these negative activities, such as killing, bullying, cheating, all these negative actions come out of this different emotion so it is real enemy. It is the destroyer of our peace, destroyer of our fortune, including our health, so therefore that's the enemy, real enemy. External enemy today may be harmful to you but next day may be very helpful. But this is the **inner enemy. This is the real destroyer of our happiness, always there.** What to do now? If there is a possibility to eliminate that, then I think now we must take this good opportunity. This is human body, human brain, human good heart. Combine these two things, try. It's to reduce that and to eventually eliminate. **The combination intelligence and emotion, that is the way to change our inner world.** So long that that enemy is there, so long we are under that enemy's control, no permanent happiness. So once you develop some kind of desire to overcome that enemy, now that is the true realization of the aspiration to seek freedom. This practice, analyzing our emotional level and our inner world is very important as the key practice."

Dalai Lama Summary

1. Help Others
2. Don't Care What Others Say
3. Pay Attention to Your Inner Values
4. Be Calm
5. Have Compassion
6. Be Determined
7. Meditate
8. Find Life's Meaning
9. Develop Friendships
10. Conquer Yourself

How can you apply these rules to your business or life today?

_____

_____

_____

_____

_____

_____

_____

_____

_____

_____

#DidYouKnow: Dalai Lama is translated as 'Ocean of Wisdom.'

"The best entrepreneurs are good communicators. It's one of the very few unifying factors." – Tim Ferriss

- Entrepreneur, author, podcaster, investor, and speaker
- His 4-Hour Workweek book has sold over 1.35 million copies
- It was rejected by 25 publishers until Random House agreed
- Called the "Oprah of Audio" from the reach of his podcast
- Was named Wired's "Greatest Self-Promoter of All Time"

Rule #1: Schedule Your Time

"Large, uninterrupted blocks of time. You have to schedule, if you are a creator, blocks of time that are *at least two to four hours* or more in length.

No Frankenstein's monster of 10 minute breaks and 20 minute breaks combined into three hours, will have the value of an uninterrupted block of three hours. We all have the same 24 hours in the day. *If you don't have time, you don't have priorities."*

Rule #2: Be Able to Sell

"You need to be able to sell. Whether it's Kickstarter, New York Times, your local newspaper. You need to be able to communicate effectively and sell. Which is why, when entrepreneurs ask me for books to read outside of business books, I say 'On Writing Well,' 'Bird by Bird,' all books on writing, improving communication. David Ogilvy, 'Ogilvy on Advertising.' Study print ads, where you have very little space. I think those are all very very effective.

The best entrepreneurs I've ever met are all good communicators. It's the one, perhaps one of the very few, unifying factors. They're exceptional communicators. Practice is the only way to get better at communicating. One of the things that I did for years is, anytime I bought something, I would identify the ad, the phone call, the print ad, the offer, whatever it was that made me decide to buy it, and I would either cut it out, or record it, put it into Evernote, whatever it might be, and save it.

So I had a record of everything that I bought and why I bought it. And then I could go back and review it and I'd be like, 'Oh, looks like I fell for this this and this,' not in a bad way, but it looks like this tipped me from, 'Eh,' or not interested to, 'Yeah I'll spend five, 50, 500, 5000 dollars on that.' I save all that. Everything that works in sales has been done already. *Just keep track of the crap that you buy, or the awesome stuff that you buy, and decide what was the trigger, what pushed me over the edge?* And then just sell to people like you. That's what I do. It's really easy. It makes it a lot easier than trying to guess."

Rule #3: Learn the Art of the Pitch

"When you're thinking about a product launch, the first thing I would ask is, '*Is it the right time* to be product launching?' So if your product isn't figured out, if you can't fill the orders, now is not the right time to be in 'TechCrunch.'

Once you're in a major media outlet, they're not going to cover you again, for some period of time, or ever. If you're in the business section of the 'New York Times,' they're not going to cover you four weeks later when your product is better and you're ready. So **make sure that you pick your timing**. There's paid exposure and unpaid exposure. I like to focus on unpaid because it forces you to make better decisions in the beginning. I would read, as I always say, 'The 22 Immutable Laws of Marketing,' '1000 True Fans' written by Kevin Kelly.

I would also read 'Bestselling Book PR and Publicity.' All of the techniques apply to more than books. **And learn to tell the story.** What are you focusing on? Are you using yourself to tell the story, and then the product is associated. Is it a trend piece? Are you trying to tie what you're doing into a greater trend, which is a very effective way of getting media. In which case, you're going to need other examples.

You need to get comfortable bringing in cooperative competitors to create that trend piece. Learn the art of the pitch and of messaging. Only once you have figured that out then you go out and you pay to acquire people, because now *if your messaging is off, it's costing you money.*"

Rule #4: Scratch Your Own Itch *[Evan's Fav]*

"I only invest in things that I understand and things that I use or would use myself. This is really really really important. Anytime I step outside of that, is usually when the universe kicks me in the nuts really hard, and I lose my money. I think it's critical to, as an entrepreneur, scratch your own itch. **It increases the odds of success or the probability of success.** And as an investor, I look for people who are scratching their own itch."

Rule #5: Let Small Bad Things Happen

"In a world where people expect immediate responses, oftentimes, and increasingly so, you have to, I believe, *let small bad things happen, constantly, to have any agenda of your own,* and to get the big positive things done.

So it's recognizing that to prevent all hurt feelings, all mistakes, all problems, all of this, is impossible.

And if you try to do that you'll *never have a proactive schedule of your own.* It's extremely important.

So effectively just saying, 'I'm going to accept the collateral damage and believe that what I'm embarking upon is *worth more than those minor or reversible problems.'*

And then forging ahead.

That's it. You got to take a few flesh wounds."

Rule #6: Ideas Are Worth Nothing

"*Ideas are worth nothing.* They're not a dime a dozen. They're just nothing. All the good founders I know, even the bad founders, can come up with ideas all day long. It doesn't mean anything.

You have to be able to execute. If an entrepreneur should, say, start a business based on one of their passions or if they should find the most attractive market opportunity and build a business out of that, whether they like it or not.

I think you need both. I would say, look at your credit card statement. Identify where you spend an unusual percentage of your income. Were you price-insensitive? Then how old are you? What gender are you? Where do you live?

And design a product that has all of those things intersected."

Rule #7: Pick the Right Things to Do

"It's very easy to be seduced by doing things efficiently, trying to do a lot of things well. I don't believe that's the most important thing. The most important thing is **picking the right things to do in the first place.** And that's being effective versus just being efficient.

So within a start up, success, I don't think is measured by how many things you can do at once. It's measured by how effectively you're able to pick one or two things that are the highest priority.

And there's always going to be a seduction to get distracted and focus on 20 things at once.

And the most effective entrepreneurs I know are **very good at focusing on one or two things** and either eliminating the rest or delegating to other people or outsourcing it so it's not done within the team but it's actually to third parties."

Rule #8: Be Pragmatically Pessimistic

"First-time entrepreneurs tend to miscalculate everything. What I mean by that is optimism has a place, but I think, even more so for the first-time entrepreneur, you need to be **pragmatically pessimistic.**

What I mean by that is you need to **define all the worst-case scenarios** in terms of financial loss, time loss, et cetera. Look at what you will learn if that happens and accept and come to terms with that before you ever start.

If you don't do that, and you go straight into battling the world, trying to conquer the world with rose-colored glasses on, the first time you hit a major hiccup, you're going to become really demoralized and you will quit.

So optimism, all that rah rah rah, that's awesome, but you need to hope for the best and prepare for the worst before you ever get started. I always recommend that."

Rule #9: Have a Focused Metric

"I think it's important to have one or two numbers that you track on a weekly basis so that could be for web-based properties, or services, or products. *Having a metric that you try to improve every week.*

You can *have one or two of them.*

You really shouldn't have many more than that.

Could be conversion from sign up, to first stage of sign up, to completion of sign up.

There are many different metrics that you can use, but I think that to keep the team focused, especially in a small company, it's very important to have one or two that you focus on a weekly basis."

Rule #10: Use Failure to Help You

"I view failure differently than, I think, many people. *I view it as a feedback mechanism.* But if you look at 'The Four Hour Workweek,' it didn't start off called 'The Four Hour Workweek.'

It was also turned down by 26 out of 27 publishers.

And hopefully pretty soon it will be celebrating four years unbroken on the New York Times best-seller list.

And I like to, whenever possible, illustrate those failures because everyone will face failure or mistakes.

And those are the divergent points from which they can either go in a good direction or a bad direction.

And I want to illustrate that *oftentimes the finish line is only 100 feet from where you stand, but it might seem that it's 100 miles away.*"

Tim Ferriss Summary

1. Schedule Your Time
2. Be Able to Sell
3. Learn the Art of the Pitch
4. Scratch Your Own Itch
5. Let Small Bad Things Happen
6. Ideas Are Worth Nothing
7. Pick the Right Things to Do
8. Be Pragmatically Pessimistic
9. Have a Focused Metric
10. Use Failure to Help You

How can you apply these rules to your business or life today?

_____

_____

_____

_____

_____

_____

_____

_____

_____

_____

_____

_____

#DidYouKnow: Tim Ferriss has been an angel investor / advisor to Facebook, Twitter, StumbleUpon, Evernote, Uber, among others.

"Spend the interest, never the principal. If everything blows up, you're okay." – Kevin O'Leary

- Investor, journalist, writer, and television personality
- Known for his blunt advice on the TV series 'Shark Tank'
- Built The Learning Company, sold it making him millions
- Founded O'Leary Funds and has over $1 billion of assets
- Known as "Mr. Wonderful" on 'Shark Tank'

Rule #1: You Have to Sacrifice

"I tried working for somebody when I was very young and they fired me and it affected me profoundly and I just said, 'I'm never working for anybody again.'

It doesn't mean your life is easier, in fact you have to have *a lot of sacrifices on the road to success* and a lot of failures along the way. I just find it a more interesting way to spend your time and I really believe in this concept of money buys freedom.

I think it's a very noble pursuit for some percentage of the people out there, but not for everybody, because you have to sacrifice a lot for the period that you're working on your business, and *not everybody wants to do that.*

I think you find that on your own, you start down that path, and if it's too much of a sacrifice you revert back to being an employee.

It's very noble to do that too, but it's not the same thing. It takes a long time to set yourself free working for somebody else."

Rule #2: Trust Your Gut *[Evan's Fav]*

"I was with a bunch of other investors who I respect and they brought me a deal and I wanted to be part of it, *but it didn't feel right.* And I wrote millions of dollars on that one and it just didn't feel right and I lost it all within two years.

Absolutely trust your gut.

This is a barometer of risk. It's something internalized for an investor that says, 'I don't feel comfortable.' It's not about emotion, it's just, don't write that check! That was recently the first time I didn't listen to that and I lost everything.

So now my radar is up. I listen to my gut. *It's not an emotion. It's an index of risk and you get it as you age.* You become a better investor every year. If only I could live to 200, I'd be really good."

Rule #3: Have Diversification

"Diversification. What I've learned that works if you're an investor, no matter how much money you've got, whether it's $5,000 or $500 million, *diversification is what saves you from disaster,* having investments in a wide range of businesses and sectors.

There's always something working when something else isn't. So, today I can go to bed tonight knowing that I have one objective: I want to go to bed richer than I woke up and the only way that's going to happen to me is to be invested in a lot of different things. Because everyday one thing works while three others don't, but sometimes that's why you get richer.

What I find people do is they fall in love with one idea or one stock or one investment or their sister comes in and says, 'I want to open a restaurant.' You should never do that. What you should say is, 'Whatever money I've got, I'll never put more than 5% into one idea. I'll never let myself get caught up in an idea that ends up being so big to me, that if it fails I get wiped out.' This is the key to success. *No more than 5% in any one idea and no more than 20%* in any one sector. For example, if you love energy stocks, only 20% max. If you love gold, only 20% max. You have to have diversification. This is the one thing that will save your heinie."

Rule #4: Have a Backup Plan

"You should make the assumption when you make an investment, there's some probability you'll lose it. It'll go to zero. And that's why you *need to have a reserve, a backup plan, some cash set aside that if everything blows up, you're okay.*

I find it extraordinary when people make their first liquidity event and they have some capital, that they blow it all again. That is the biggest mistake. You've got to take a nut, even if it stays in cash, or it's a very, very liquid safe security to say, 'That, I don't touch.' It goes back to what my mother taught me, *'Spend the interest, never the principal.'* I mean look, I make a lot of crazy investments. I don't touch the principal."

Rule #5: Be a Leader

"Communication skills are paramount. The ability to actually articulate what your idea is in a very short period of time is number one. Number two, just because you have a good idea, doesn't mean you're going to make money. There's a difference between a good idea and someone *who can execute the business plan.* So you spend the next five minutes of your presentation explaining why you're the right person to actually execute the plan. Whether it's on 'Shark Tank' or else somewhere else. You have to go through that gauntlet to prove that you're the right person or your team are the right people. And if those two things come together, then the magic starts. That's when a team or a person starts to sizzle like an isotope, because clearly they've become a leader. It's clear that they're different than everybody else. *Not only can they articulate their idea, they can actually convince you they can execute it."*

Rule #6: Admit Your Weakness

"The reason most people fail in business is they *make the assumption they're good at everything.* And they're egotistical maniacs and even when it starts to fail because of their own inadequacies they don't stop themselves and they blow up. That's a typical situation for an entrepreneur. So you have to look yourself in the mirror, and this is hard to do sometimes, and say, 'What am I really good at and what do I suck at?' *Because you don't want to spend any of your time doing things you're no good at.* If you've got a software company you have to make 10 million discs a month and you don't like that, you better find a guy who knows how to do that, and you better make him your partner very early on in the process. And I mean partner. I mean you give him something. You give equity up to fulfill the weaknesses in your own portfolio. That is the key to success. I will never make any money by myself, ever. I've sold many businesses now. Started many. Failed at many. The only ones I've really made money from are partnerships where I found people that were good at things that I wasn't good at. I don't mean employees. I mean giving them equity in the business so that they have the *same risks and desires that I have."*

Rule #7: Buy Stocks with Dividends

"I remembered a story, really affected me years ago. My mother, she'd always invest a third of her paycheck into Bell bonds with coupons. She'd always say to me, 'Boys, never spend the principal, just the interest. And never ever, ever, ever buy a security that doesn't pay a dividend.' Back in those days stocks paid higher dividends than the bonds. So example, Bell Canada had a six percent yield on its five year bonds. The stock yielded seven to entice people to take the risk to own an equity.

We got lost somewhere between the 50s and the 60s and 70s, and we actually thought that it was a good investment to buy a stock that didn't pay a dividend, which to me is insane. So I wanted to found a firm on that, my mother's basic concept because, she died a few years ago and I was executor for her state and I looked at her portfolio, which she never shared with anybody. But 40 years, compounded dividends and bonds, 73% of the market returns in the *last 40 years came from dividends* not capital appreciation, and she knew that intuitively.

That's how we built the foundation of O'Leary Funds. We listened to mom. We don't own a single security that doesn't pay a dividend. *I will never buy a stock in my life that doesn't pay a dividend.* If it's not returning cash to me, it's a speculation, and if a manager can't send me cash, I'm not interested."

Rule #8: Differentiate Between Family, Friends and Money

"Often, your family will come to you, your cousin, your uncle, your sister saying, 'Please, invest in my business.' You've got to differentiate between family, friends and money. You've got to be careful that you don't get yourself in a situation where you lose your money because you got *emotionally involved.*

That's a very big piece of advice, because I've done it. Everybody's made mistakes as an investor. That's one of the ones I made in the early times I never make again."

Rule #9: Get Outside of North America

"I tell every entrepreneur to try and get, **over the next five years, 30% of your sales outside of North America.** The whole idea is you diversify your sales risk. You diversify your portfolio. If you're just selling in the US, you're going to be selling to an economy that's growing at sub 3% for the rest of your life."

Rule #10: Go with Simple Ideas

"So, Oprah has a hairdresser. Interesting guy. His hobby was tea. This tea you drink and he became what's called a 'Nose.' He had a certain skill to be able to smell teas and blend them. One day he gives a cup of tea to Oprah while he's doing her hair, and she sips it and says, 'This is the best tea I've ever had!' She goes on the show a half an hour later and says, 'This tea, called Talbot Teas is the best tea I've ever had.' He gets orders the next day for $500,000.

You know, the 'Oprah Effect,' you've heard of it right? He can't finance that. So he comes on 'Shark Tank' and he's looking for $250,000 and I agree to buy 35% of the company for that. I love tea. It's so simple. Gets on 'Oprah', 5,000 orders, Neiman Marcus, all kinds of individuals ordering on the Internet.

Simple. Tea, orders, cash flow right? While we're in the middle of doing the deal, the show airs and Jamba Juice, a public company says we want to be in the tea business. We love this story, we love the brand, I want to buy the company.

I haven't even written the check yet and bang, the deal's done. That's the kind of deal I like, because it was simple. It's not a complicated tech story. It's tea. Tea with a brand. Now you go into a Jamba Juice anywhere in North America, that's my Talbot Teas.

I look at it this way, the **simple deals are the the ones you make money on.** So I take that cash back. I redeploy it. So I like simple stories with revenue attached to them. The high tech stuff, I came out of that market. It's so complicated. So much can go wrong. I just love deals where they see an easy path to revenue."

Kevin O'Leary Summary

1. You Have to Sacrifice
2. Trust Your Gut
3. Have Diversification
4. Have a Backup Plan
5. Be a Leader
6. Admit Your Weaknesses
7. Buy Stocks with Dividends
8. Differentiate Between Family, Friends, and Money
9. Get Outside of North America
10. Go with Simple Ideas

How can you apply these rules to your business or life today?

_____

_____

_____

_____

_____

_____

_____

_____

_____

_____

#DidYouKnow: In 2017 he campaigned to be the political leader of the Conservative Party of Canada.

"The more responsibility you have in your life, more is the need for meditation."
– Sri Sri Ravi Shankar

- Spiritual leader and founder of the Art of Living Foundation
- Aims to reduce stress, societal problems, and violence
- Teaches that spirituality enhances human values
- Received Padma Vibhushan, India's Second Highest Award
- Named by Forbes as the 5th most powerful leader in India

Rule #1: Welcome Constructive Criticism

"I'm one who always welcomes criticism.

I encourage people, you should welcome criticism.

And be **bold enough to give criticism.**

If the criticism is coming out of benevolence that someone is criticizing me so that I can become better, then it is always welcome.

But if someone is criticizing just out of jealousy or trying to pull someone down, then that is not good.

Then that is coming from a malefic mindset.

So constructive criticism, I feel everyone should welcome.

Criticism, compassion. Criticism with love is most adorable thing and it should always be welcomed."

Rule #2: Get Out of Your Comfort Zone [Evan's Fav]

"If you can **embrace embarrassment,** nothing can shake you.

It's one thing that people try to run away from is embarrassment.

Embarrassment is a mild form of criticism.

A mild form of feeling uncomfortable.

So sometimes, we need to get out of the comfort zone, feel that little uncomfortable.

Yes, then, abilities in us dawn."

Rule #3: Be Stable, Still, and Content

"If you are content, happy. *If you're centered, everything will flow to you.* You don't have to go and grab something. Things will come your way. This is what I'm saying. This is why this world is called, 'Maya.'

Do you know what Maya means? When you try to go and grab it, it runs away from you. If you try to possess it, you try to grab something, it just runs away.

And *if you are stable, still, content within yourself, they all run towards you."*

Rule #4: Learn from Everyone

"You know I say we are all global people. *We have to learn something from every way in the world.*

And I would say we have to learn the precision, and the timeliness, and the commitment from Germans. The world should learn. I always say that perfection is always Germans.

Etiquette is always from England. The mannerisms, etiquettes, you know? And business and salesmanship, Americans. Teamwork from Japanese. Japanese are so good in teamwork.

Similarly, spirituality from India. Human values, spirituality, compassion. It all comes from India.

So we need to *get the best from every part of the world.* In the next coming generation we'll see that sort of global human being. Of course, technology has shrunk the whole world into a global village.

Today through technology, once again, we communicate with the whole world. In the same way, if we can tune our minds to the simplicities, the innocence, to caring and sharing, we will find the whole world as one family. Global family."

Rule #5: Create Balance in Your Life

"When you want to have balance, you will definitely have it. You can have it. 'I want to have balance my life.' This thought itself is good enough. You're already balancing. You are moving in the direction. This question simply arises, 'How do I do it?' You know you can do it. Ask yourself. *Your consciousness will tell you.* Listen to your consciousness. If you're attending to your work too much, your consciousness will prick, 'Hey you're forgetting your family, your wife, your children, your husband.'

If you're attending too much in the family, and forget about all other things, then your consciousness will prick, 'My God, what did I get into? Day and night I'm just immerged in family affairs, I'm not being useful to the world. I have to do something. I have to pursue my cause. I have to do justice to my work.' *The mind will prick.* Then you'll do that. But this wanting to keep balance in life, that very thought is good enough.

A little bit of guilt is okay. But not too much. Like salt in the food. If there is too much salt, can you eat it? No. Got it? So wanting to have balance is good to have."

Rule #6: Passion, Dispassion, Compassion

"Like breathing in and breathing out we need passion, we need dispassion, and we need compassion. All three have to exist. People without passion cannot achieve anything in their life. So you need passion. Especially youngsters, they need to have a passion. *They lack passion, they get into depression.* So passion is essential.

But only passion, this has been the problem. Only passion will lead to disappointment and despair. So you *need to have little detachment,* that is dispassion. And dispassion is when it's like, 'Okay you did a lot of activity and you take some time to sleep, rest.' You let everything go and relax. You switch over to this side, and *meditation* is part of it. The ability to let go and move forward, that I would call as dispassion. And in between we need compassion."

215

Rule #7: Weigh the Pros and Cons

"If you see you have a **wrong decision,** you have to weigh the pros and cons.

'Should I continue in this all my life? Or should I change? If I change what is the loss that I will face? What are the problems I may encounter?'

You have to weigh it. You have to see how much the change will make you better or if the change is even more problematic, better not change.

Just carry on with whatever wrong decision you made. Sometimes you can't change. You have made a wrong decision. You have to go.

You can't think of being a bachelor after you have had a kid. Once you have a child, then you have to be a father or mother and continue.

There's no point in regretting the past.

Similarly, you wanted to be a doctor, but you became an engineer. And after 25 years of serving as an engineer, you can't say, 'No I made a wrong choice. I should've been a doctor.'

There's no point.

Now you can't go back to study at school and become a doctor, again.

You are an engineer, continue on with that. Got it? So you have to weigh the pros and cons."

Rule #8: You Have to Put Effort Into It

"To achieve anything in the world, it **needs effort.** To achieve anything in the world, any pleasure or any material thing you want to achieve, it needs effort."

SRI SRI RAVI SHANKAR

Rule #9: Meditate

"If you look at the benefits that meditation bring into our life, you feel it is all the more relevant, all the more needed.

In ancient times meditation was used for enlightenment.

For finding the self.

And meditation is a way to get rid of misery, to overcome misery, overcome problems.

Meditation has been the way to improve one's abilities.

And today, if you see the social ills of today, the stress and tension, it calls for one to meditate.

The more responsibility you have in your life, more is the need for meditation."

Rule #10: Life is Much Larger than Failure and Success

"Life is much larger than failure and success.

Life is much larger than birth and death.

We are much beyond them all.

Got it?

If you have the strength, if you can understand this knowledge, then you will walk like a king.

Nobody can shake you."

Sri Sri Ravi Shankar Summary

1. Welcome constructive Criticism
2. Get Out of Your Comfort Zone
3. Be Stable, Still, and Content
4. Learn from Everyone
5. Create Balance in Your Life
6. Passion, Dispassion, Compassion
7. Weigh the Pros and Cons
8. You Have to Put Effort Into It
9. Meditate
10. Life Is Much Larger than Failure and Success

How can you apply these rules to your business or life today?

_____

_____

_____

_____

_____

_____

_____

_____

_____

_____

#DidYouKnow: For his service, Sri Sri Ravi Shankar has received some of the highest awards of several countries including India, Peru, Colombia, and Paraguay.

"Difficulty is an opportunity to get stronger. To develop character. To gain new confidence." – Joel Osteen

- Preacher, televangelist, and author
- Senior Pastor at Lakewood, the largest US Protestant church
- Wrote 7 New York Times Bestselling books
- Over 20 million people watch his sermons every month
- Lakewood Church services are seen in over 100 countries

Rule #1: Plant the Right Seeds

"You are where you are today in part because of what you've been saying about yourself. *Words are like seeds. When you speak something out, you give life to what you're saying.* If you continue to say it, eventually that can become a reality.

Whether you realize it or not, you are prophesying your future. And this is great when we're saying things like, 'I'm blessed, I'm strong, I will accomplish my dreams, I'm coming out of debt.' That's not just being positive. You are prophesying victory, prophesying success, prophesying new levels. *And your life will move in the direction of your words.*

But too many people go around prophesying just the opposite. 'I never get any good breaks. I'll never get back in shape. Business is slow. I'll probably get laid off. Flu season is here, I always get it.' They don't realize they are prophesying defeat. It's just like they're calling in bad breaks, mediocrity, lack.

And the Scripture says, we will eat the fruit of our words. You are planting seeds when you talk. At some point you're going to eat that fruit. My challenge is, *make sure you're planting the right kind of seeds.* If you want apples, you have to sow apple seeds."

Rule #2: Be in Peace

"You can handle it so much better when you're in the difficult times knowing that somehow it's going to work for your good. Because otherwise, you're always fighting something, 'Wow, I'm fighting. I got to get out of this job, or I don't like this marriage.'

If we don't watch it, we'll go through life fighting. When you realize nothing's happening to me, it's happening for me. So even though I'm in a difficult time, I'm going to be in peace today.

I'm going to be good to somebody because when you're in peace, *it's a position of power, and when you stay in peace,* God will get you to where you're supposed to be, will move the wrong people out of the way, open up the right doors."

Rule #3: Don't Accept Mediocrity *[Evan's Fav]*

"Don't let your mind become conditioned for mediocrity.

Don't let that change who you really are.

Sometimes, people will try to put us in a box and tell us things like, 'You can't start that business. You don't have the resources. You'll never afford a nice place to live, never get well, never meet the right person.'

Because their thinking is limited, they'll try to put their limitations on you.

You have to put your foot down and say, *'I refuse to be mediocre because people around me are mediocre.* I refuse to be addicted, depressed, have low expectations. I know I'm a barrier breaker. I'm going to set a new standard.'

It starts in our thinking.

Nothing will change until you make up your mind you are not going to accept mediocrity."

Rule #4: Invite Positive Things In

"What follows the words 'I am,' *I believe you're inviting into your life.*

So I think a lot of people don't realize it, but playing in their mind, and even sometimes we say it, 'You know what, I am slow. I am unlucky. I am not attractive.'

And I think we're inviting negative things in. I think we're supposed to say, 'You know what? I'm blessed. I'm strong, I'm healthy, I'm talented.'

You have to invite the right things into your life."

Rule #5: Don't Give Up

"A man in the lobby told me the other day how he had a dream to start his own business. He got it going, everything was fine, he was so excited.

But he hit a series of setbacks. Unfortunately, he didn't make it. He thought he was done, that it would never happen. No, it just wasn't the right time.

Don't give up. Don't let that dream die stillborn.

It may not have happened in the past, but you've come into a set time. Ideas waiting for you. The right people waiting for you. Try it again.

The Scripture says, 'A good man falls seven times, but the Lord raises him back up.' The loan didn't go through? You didn't qualify for that new house?

Try again. You're in a set time of favor. You tried to lose the weight, tried to get back in shape. It didn't work out. Try it again."

Rule #6: Stay Grounded

"I think it's a ***part of discipline.***

I think it's a part of staying grounded, and you know, one thing I've been good at, because there have been a lot of ministers like me. And you know them all.

That haven't made it long term. But I'm good about getting up every day and searching my own heart, and saying, ***'Am I on the right track?'***

And I too, I think about temptation. I realize, you come down a lot faster than you went up, and we've seen all that.

So, I just think it comes from ***keeping your own heart pure.***"

Rule #7: Let Go of the Past

"We all have had negative things happen to us. People did us wrong, the company laid us off, a clerk was rude to us. It's easy to go through life offended, in self-pity, blaming others, *blaming ourselves.*

And because we're always looking back, reliving the negative, we end up carrying around all this baggage that weighs us down. One of the best things we can learn to do is drop it. *Let it go.*

Whether it happened 20 years ago, or 20 minutes ago, don't carry negative baggage from yesterday into today.

You won't live a victorious life if you're always reliving what didn't work out, who hurt you, the mistakes you've made.

The reason it's called the past is because it's over. It's done, it's history. Now do your part and let it go.

'Well, Joel, they betrayed me, they walked away, broke my heart. That's why I'm bitter. That's why I'm upset.' *They hurt you once, don't let them continue to hurt you by always thinking about it.*"

Rule #8: Be Practical

"There's a lot of things beating people down already. I've found most people already feel guilty enough. They already know what they're doing wrong.

Not everybody, but most. So I think when our message is practical, relevant, how do I forgive? *How do I have a good attitude? How do I reach my destiny?*

I think if there's sometimes when we don't change, and it's just all doctrine, and it's just, 'I'm going to be beat down, I'm going to feel guilty.'

I think that's maybe what pulls some people away."

Rule #9: Don't Waste Your Pain

"The key is what we do in our times of pain. *Pain will change us.* Heartache, loss, disappointments, they don't leave us the same. When I lost my father, I didn't come out like I was before. I was changed. If you go through a divorce, a legal battle, a friend betrays you, eventually that will pass. You'll get through it, but you will be different. *How the pain changes you is up to you. You can come out bitter or you can come out better.* You can come out with a chip on your shoulder or you can come out stronger with greater confidence. You can come out defeated, giving up on your dreams, or you can come out with a new passion, a new fire, excited about the new opportunities in front of you. All of us experience pain. My challenge, don't just go through it, grow through it. *That difficulty is an opportunity to get stronger.* To develop character. To gain new confidence. Anybody can give up. Anybody can let it overwhelm you. But you know what that's doing? Wasting your pain. That pain is not there to stop you, *it's there to prepare you, to increase you, to develop you.*"

Rule #10: Let Your Enemies Motivate You

"In 2002, we received word that the Houston Rockets were moving out of this building and the city was selling it. When I heard that, something came alive. I knew it was supposed to be ours. A very influential man found out and said very sarcastically, 'It will be a cold day in Hell before Lakewood ever gets that building.' When I heard how against us he was, *I was already determined,* but something rose up in me. I had a holy determination. I had a new fire, a new resolve, and every time things got tough, looked like it wasn't going to work out, I would be tempted to get discouraged, I could hear that phrase, 'a cold day in Hell.' I'd get my passion right back. Wouldn't take me five seconds. That business leader that was so against us. He doesn't realize it, he was one of the most instrumental people in us getting this building. If I ever see that man, I need to buy him dinner. Some of my enemies I feel like I need to write them a check. If they hadn't have made fun, I would've given up sooner. If they hadn't have told me I couldn't do it, didn't have what it takes, I might've been complacent, settled where I was. *It was their opposition that pushed me forward.*"

Joel Osteen Summary

1. Plant the Right Seeds
2. Be in Peace
3. Don't Accept Mediocrity
4. Invite Positive Things In
5. Don't Give Up
6. Stay Grounded
7. Let Go of the Past
8. Be Practical
9. Don't Waste Your Pain
10. Let Your Enemies Motivate You

How can you apply these rules to your business or life today?

_____

_____

_____

_____

_____

_____

_____

_____

_____

_____

#DidYouKnow: Joel Osteen's first book, Your Best Life Now, debuted at the top of The New York Times Best Seller list and remained on the list for more than 200 weeks.

"My word is my bond. It's my commitment. You have to keep working if you're committed." – Priyanka Chopra

- Actress, singer, film producer, and philanthropist
- Won the Miss World 2000 pageant
- One of Time's "100 Most Influential People in the World"
- Was 1st South Asian woman to headline a US network series
- Has worked with UNICEF for the last 10 years

Rule #1: Set Goals for Yourself

"I don't want to be called an actor. I don't want to be called a star. I don't want to have a label. *I want to have a legacy.* I want to be known as someone who has goals and achieves them. And whatever they might be, wherever they might be. I want to be limitless. I want to break stereotypes. I want to go where no man or woman has gone before. And it might be a scary path. And it might be a path that no one's taken, but at least it'll be just mine. I had the worst self-esteem when I was a kid. I was made fun of because of the way I talked because of where I came from. I was made fun of on every level and the only way you can change that is setting goals for yourself and saying, *'I'll be the best version of me.'*

When I was 18 and I started doing movies I gave myself a year and a half. And I said, 'If I sense that I'm not good at what I'm doing and I don't see something opening up for me, I'm going to go back to college.' I always had a *plan B*. I still always have a plan B. And that's what I always tell young people, *that life doesn't end, it just keeps moving.* You have to put your blinkers on and find what you do best and just keep moving."

Rule #2: Don't be Conventional

"The 'exotic, beautiful, Indian girl,' it's an easier fit. I've decided never to do it. I'm doing a movie in which I'm not the sidekick. I'm the main villain of the movie, which is different. Who would debut as a villain? My first debut will be a villain, an antagonist. But to me, that strikes me as exciting. *I don't like being conventional.* I was tried to put into that box so much. That was the first place I was put into. All the movies that came to me was that. In fact Baywatch, I was being spoken to for another part. But the exotic, gorgeous, pretty girl in amazing clothes is where people tried to put me. And I hope that doesn't happen to anyone else coming in because it'll really ruin all the work I've done. *We need to stand as a force to reckon with.* We need to not be afraid to stand our ground on our feet and say, 'I'm not settling.' I hope that Indian talent comes in and does that and I hope that me being in the position that I am in can give them the confidence to do it."

Rule #3: Create Your Own Path

"What is the choice?

That you walk a path **like everyone else,** dressed in suits, go to work, and come back, and never have a legacy?

Or you swim upstream like a trout **against the norm** and then whatever little you achieve is only yours?

It's not like everyone else.

I'd rather have something that is **my path,** paved by me.

Something that is my legacy, my own self, my own achievement rather than being one of the many successful people in the world."

Rule #4: #Believe in Yourself *[Evan's Fav]*

"'Quantico' was my first audition. I knew I had to go into this room and read these lines in front of all these people.

But I was so nervous before I went in.

So I went to the bathroom.

I remember, before I went in, and looked in the mirror, and it's so stupid and cliché, **I talked to myself,** and I said, 'What's wrong with you?

You've played the most difficult characters in the most complicated movies.'

I tossed my hair a little bit, felt great, and walked out. Did my bit, and got the job."

Rule #5: Have Boundaries

"Nudity. *I wouldn't do it.* Like never. I play bold parts.

But I don't like a lot of skin shown. I don't know how to explain it. Like in 'Aitraaz,' I was always in pantsuits. But the intensity, and the part was sexual, I didn't have to dress it.

I mean I would do it for a magazine cover here and there because it's glamorous and it's pretty.

One of the big reasons why I did the show with ABC was because they're Disney.

There's a difference between wearing a bikini and a bra and I understand that. *And those lines are important to me."*

Rule #6: Don't Limit Yourself

"I'm a storyteller.

And I'm not someone who *restricts myself to one thing.*

Ever.

I've never been that person.

Maybe I have ADD, but *I want to be able to do everything.* Why can't we do everything?

And especially women, we're great at multitasking. So I want to produce, I want to have a business, I'm producing here, I'm going to produce in India, Hindi films, regional films.

I want to be able to act in them. There's so many things that I can do, which I want to be able to explore."

Rule #7: Be an Achiever

"I don't consider myself a singer. I don't consider myself an actor. *I consider myself an achiever.* You can give me anything.

You tell me to paint the walls of the studio and I'll do the best damn painting job you've ever seen.

That's how I've always been. I didn't know I was going to be an actress.

I didn't know I was going to be a musician. But now, whatever opportunities I get I'm trying turn them to, 'Let's see what will happen.'

Hard work is something I know I can damn well do.

I want to expand myself as an entertainer as a performer.

Whether that's music. Whether that's TV. Whether that's films. Whether that's production. Anything."

Rule #8: Stay Committed

"People don't think I'm ever tired. It's only because all the stuff that I have to do is what I need to do. I don't have time for unnecessary work between two continents.

My word is my bond. It's my commitment. I'm professional. My inherent nature is that you have to keep working if you're committed to something.

My mum used to say this to me, 'As a woman, no one should see the chinks in your armor because it is only your own.'

We're strong because we have the ability as women to be able to hold on to a lot of emotions.

A lot of things that are thrown at us but we just have to remember that, *'Don't let the world see your weakness.'"*

Rule #9: Don't be Afraid to Dream

"The most beautiful thing about having dreams is that it's *in your hands how big your dreams become.*

I've come here only to introduce you to the idea of saying that no one can tell you that your dream is too small!

Or your dream can't come true.

Or your dream can't be allowed because you're a girl, because you're a boy, because you look a certain way, or because you come from a certain place.

Don't be afraid to dream because they do come true.

They really do."

Rule #10: Become Irreplaceable

"When I was very young, I was 19 and I was doing the first few movies, I remember the producer just said, 'Well, if she can't work it out, it's fine, we'll just cast someone else.

Girls are replaceable.'

Subconsciously, it really worked on my mind and I started picking up parts which were strong, which were not just the damsel in distress waiting for someone to rescue me.

Now 13 to 15 years later, *the movies I do, I'm irreplaceable.*"

Priyanka Chopra Summary

1. Set Goals for Yourself
2. Don't be Conventional
3. Create Your Own Path
4. #Believe in Yourself
5. Have Boundaries
6. Don't Limit Yourself
7. Be an Achiever
8. Stay Committed
9. Don't be Afraid to Dream
10. Become Irreplaceable

How can you apply these rules to your business or life today?

_____

_____

_____

_____

_____

_____

_____

_____

_____

_____

_____

_____

#DidYouKnow: In 2016, the Government of India honored Priyanka Chopra with the Padma Shri, the 4th highest civilian award.

"I am a human being and I have a future and I can go to bed feeling strong and full of hope." – Nelson Mandela

- Anti-apartheid revolutionary, politician, and philanthropist
- Served as President of South Africa from 1994 to 1999
- Described as the "Father of the Nation" in South Africa
- Spent 27 years in jail, a global campaign lobbied his release
- Received over 250 honors, including the Nobel Peace Prize

Rule #1: Use Your Time Wisely

"I hated oppression and when I think about the past, the type of things they did, *I feel angry.*

You have a *limited time to stay on Earth.*

You must try and use that period for the pebbles of transforming your country into what you desire it to be."

Rule #2: Prove Them Wrong

"When I found some place in my country, and a lady inside the telephone I then asked, 'To whom am I speaking?'

She said, 'You're speaking to me.' I said, 'Well, lady, I know I am speaking to you but what's your name?'

She said, 'Who are you to ask for my name? What's your name?' I said, 'Well, lady, as soon as you tell me your name, I'll tell you mine.'

But as we argued as to who should tell his or her name, she became very cross. And she said, 'You seem to be a backward person. *Have you passed your matric?'*

Now, a matric our country is a university re-examination.

And I said, 'Well, lady, you must be very careful because if the qualification to speak to you is the possession of a matric certificate I might work hard and pass my matric and be in the same class as you are.'

That was treason. She said, 'You will never be in my class,' and banged the telephone.

How I wish she were here today.

She would now discover that *I have achieved more than pass my matric."*

Rule #3: Demand Respect *[Evan's Fav]*

Oprah Winfrey: "How did you get the racist guards to treat you with respect?

You were in prison and you said I will only respond to the name Mandela or Mr. Mandela."

Nelson Mandela: ***"You must fight the battle for dignity.***

On the very first day you go to jail.

And that's what we did.

We put our foot down and insisted in being respected even though we're prisoners.

And we, thankfully, succeeded in that."

Rule #4: Make Your Enemy Your Partner

"We could not affect a peaceful transformation without talking to our enemy, addressing their fears as a minority, and the trauma of losing power.

It was under those circumstances that reconciliation took place in South Africa.

We would therefore expect the ruling majority to take the initiative to ensure that the feelings of that minority are addressed, and that programs of upliftment are made available to them.

If you want to make peace with your enemy, **you have to work with your enemy.**

Then he becomes your partner."

Rule #5: Be Humble

"The first thing is to be *honest with yourself.*

You can never have an impact on society if you have not changed yourself.

And one of the most important weapons in changing yourself is to recognize that peace, *people everywhere in the world want peace.*

But humility is one of the most important qualities which you must have because if you are humble, if you *make people realize that you are no threat for them, then people will embrace you.*

They will listen to you."

Rule #6: Have Heroes

Interviewer: "Was Muhammad Ali a hero of yours?"

Nelson Mandela: "Well, naturally.

As far as boxing is concerned and what he has done, he was my hero."

Interviewer: "So what leaders of the 20th Century do you admire?"

Nelson Mandela: "It's the not question of a leader.

It's a question of a human being *who does something to make an ordinary individual to feel, 'I am a human being' and 'I have a future' and 'I can go to bed feeling strong and full of hope.'*"

Rule #7: Lead From Behind

"It is better to **lead from behind and to put others in front,** especially when you celebrate victory when nice things occur.

You **take the front line when there is danger.**

Then people will appreciate your leadership.

As a leader, I have always followed the principles I first saw demonstrated by the regent at the Great Place.

I have always endeavored to **listen to what each and every person** in a discussion had to say before venturing my own opinion.

Oftentimes, my own opinion will simply represent a consensus of what I heard in the discussion.

I always remember the regent's axiom: 'A leader,' he said, 'is like a shepherd.

He stays behind the flock, letting the most nimble go out ahead, whereupon the others follow, not realizing that **all along they are being directed from behind.'"

Rule #8: Manage Your Emotions

"**Our emotions** said the white minority is an enemy.

We must never talk to them.

But our brain said if you don't talk to this man, your country will go up in flames.

And, for many years to come, this country would be engulfed in rivers of blood.

So we had to **reconcile that conflict and our talking to the enemy was the result of the domination of the brain over emotions.**"

Rule #9: Be Willing to Die for Your Cause

Interviewer: "You were convicted in 1964 for conspiracy against the state and, when you pleaded, you said that, *'I am willing to die for this cause.'* This is a very tough thing to say."

Nelson Mandela: "Yes, I had to say that. Not from a spirit of bravado but because I genuinely felt that they were going to hang us. And it is the desire of every freedom fighter to disappear under a cloud of glory rather than that of shame.

It is the task of a freedom fighter, when you see that the end of your days has come, to leave a tradition of bravery, determination. To face even death for your principles.

And, I thought about it. It was not because I was brave but because one had a *duty to perform at that moment.*

I have dedicated my life to this struggle of the African people. I have fought against white domination and I have fought against black domination.

I have cherished the idea of a democratic and free society in which all persons will *live together in harmony* and with equal opportunities. It is an idea for which I hope to live for and to see realized. But my Lord, if it needs be, it is an idea for which I am prepared to die."

Rule #10: Be Consistent

"Anybody who changes his principles, depending on whom he is dealing, *that is not a man who can lead a nation.*

I have refused to be drawn into the differences that exist between various communities inside the USA.

Why are you so keen that I should involve myself in the internal affairs of Cuba and Libya?

I expect you to be consistent."

Nelson Mandela Summary

1. Use Your Time Wisely
2. Prove Them Wrong
3. Demand Respect
4. Make Your Enemy Your Partner
5. Be Humble
6. Have Heroes
7. Lead From Behind
8. Manage Your emotions
9. Be Willing to Die for Your Cause
10.   Be Consistent

How can you apply these rules to your business or life today?

_____

_____

_____

_____

_____

_____

_____

_____

_____

_____

_____

#DidYouKnow: Nelson Mandela refused to drink alcohol or smoke, and even as President made his own bed.

"Be on time. Know what you're doing. Do it full out. Give all you can. That's a lesson." – Morgan Freeman

- Actor, producer, narrator known for his smooth, deep voice
- Won an Academy Award for Best Supporting Actor
- Ranked as the 4th highest box office star
- At age 12, he won a statewide drama competition
- Gained fame playing chauffeur Hoke in Driving Miss Daisy

Rule #1: Prioritize Education

Interviewer: "Why this show, [Through The Wormhole]?

On top of being an actor, a producer, a director, a philosopher as well?"

Morgan Freeman: "This is a teaching opportunity, and I'm all for that.

I think that education is one of our major shortcomings today.

We must inspire them, we must teach them, and the younger we can start, the better."

Rule #2: Build Word of Mouth

"The box office success when 'The Shawshank Redemption' came out was 'Dumb and Dumber.'

That's the juxtaposition of box office.

Shawshank got really good reviews, but because nobody could say 'Shawshank Redemption,' it didn't get word of mouth.

And I don't care how much you promote a film, if you don't have *word of mouth*, you ain't promoting it.

People have to be able to go and say, *'Listen, I saw this really terrific film, it was called, Shanksham... Shimshunk.'*

Got on the elevator in L.A. one day and the lady said, 'Oh, I just saw you in the Hudsucker Reduction.'

So, that was the reason it was not a box office success.

No word of mouth at all."

Rule #3: Be Courageous *[Evan's Fav]*

Interviewer: "Here's a stat, the richest 85 people on this planet have as much money as the poorest 3.5 billion. When you say the 'Pull yourself up by the bootstraps' thing, you're just being respectable. Not everybody can do that."

Morgan Freeman: "Bull****, everybody can.

Everybody doesn't.

Courage, courage is the key to life itself.

There are a lot of people who are born in situations where they say, 'Well, I'll never get out of this,' so, they won't.

I say to people who say, 'Well, I would like to have done so and so, so and so,' and I say, 'Well, you could've done it.'

They say, 'Well, I couldn't get out of here,' 'Well, man, the bus runs every day.'

If you can think of it, you can do it.

That's the human condition.

If we can imagine it, we can do it.

I think that's the condition of each individual human."

Rule #4: Stick with it

"I think you have to have the idea in your head that ***you're going to succeed.***

Otherwise you drive a truck.

I always felt that I was going to stick with it ***until I got it done."***

Rule #5: Show Your Ability

"I feel very secure in my person-hood, you know?

I mean **I've always felt secure in my ability,** but you don't know if anyone else sees your ability right off.

I've had directors tell me to do stuff on screen, that I knew was wrong, and you try to tell them, ' That's not right.'

So rather than create a schism, say, **'OK I'll do one for you, and I'll do one for me.'**

And if they do that, and they see it on the big screen, they come back and they'll tell you, **'You were right.'**"

Rule #6: Learn from Others

"The first stage play I did in New York, I was working with Stacy Keach. That was a great experience for me. You talk about a master class, you have it there.

Stacy had come out of Yale University, I think, and he was much more advanced as a stage actor than I was, but wow, did **I have big ears, and was I ready to learn.**

So, you just sit and watch. It's always a learning experience.

The big thing I learned from working with Pearl Bailey was professionalism.

She was a total professional. Total, total, total professional. She **always gave 100%, 110% in a performance.** And I watched her very carefully.

She was one of those performers that you say, 'This is the way to go. This is the way to be, in this business.'

Be on time. Know what you're doing. Do it full out. Give all you can. That's a lesson."

Rule #7: Find Your Path

"I got into the air force because I was romanticizing that whole idea, we were re-fighting World War II.

As I was growing up we had all these heroic movies and I fell in love with the idea of flying.

And, then, when I got into the air force, I had this big eye opener, that racism was rampant there also, and that I am **not as suited for military life,** that kind of, unquestioning obedience to a lot of things that I think are stupid, didn't quite go over well.

So, when I got out, I was an early discharge. It was almost dishonorable because I just really didn't fit, but the catalyst was in a jet trainer.

I had a lot of people behind me to get me into flight school, but sitting there, it occurred to me that this is **absolutely not what I want.** It isn't movies, it's for real, you know, this little red button on the joystick controls. Guns with real bullets.

I sat there for quite a while and knew.

So, I got out of that plane, on the runway, at North Island Air Station, a Naval air station, and **I walked away from that and towards acting. I knew that it was all about the movies. It was all about the movies."**

Rule #8: Always Do Your Best

"Your job is to **give it your best shot every time.**

I'm going into it with the idea that I'll play it to the best of my ability.

They wouldn't give me the role if they didn't think I was capable of pulling it off.

I wouldn't take it if I didn't think I was **capable of pulling it off."**

Rule #9: Hold On to Your Values

"I went to the movies all the time. I've seen the movies, and at some point it struck me rather dramatically, how much I wasn't in the movies. Not the way I needed to be in the movies.

And, if you look at a lot of the disaster movies in that period, the only people left on the planet were white. So now, my thing is if I get in the movies, I want to make sure, that I speak about that.

That if I am able to do it, I want to talk about it. So, there was a period there in the early 80's, when *I didn't get any work because I would ask these questions.*

I interviewed for the movie, 'The Thing,' the remake. I read the script, and I go back for the audition, and the producer or the director said, 'Did you read the script?', I said, 'Yes.' 'What did you think?'

I said, 'Well, you've got 11 people at the South Pole, eight of them are scientists, and then you have a cook, a mechanic. And something else. *They're all black, none of the scientists are. What do you think I think?'*

Needless to say, I didn't get that job. Again though, providence rears her beautiful head, when 'Glory' came about.

We could ask ourselves. We, me, black people. Why don't we figure more in it? I need something that's going to engage me, that makes me sit up and think. *I refuse to take part in anything that is going to denigrate a people. Especially me."*

Rule #10: Keep Going

"I always tell my kids, 'If you lay down, people will step over you. But if you keep scrambling, *if you keep going, someone will always, always give you a hand.*

Always. But you gotta keep dancing. You gotta keep moving your feet.'"

Morgan Freeman Summary

1. Prioritize Education
2. Build Word of Mouth
3. Be Courageous
4. Stick with it
5. Show Your Ability
6. Learn from Others
7. Find Your Path
8. Always Do Your Best
9. Hold On to Your Values
10. Keep Going

How can you apply these rules to your business or life today?

_____

_____

_____

_____

_____

_____

_____

_____

_____

_____

_____

_____

#DidYouKnow: Morgan Freeman earned a private pilot's license at age 65.

"It's about how hard you can get hit, and keep moving forward. That's how winning is done!" – Sylvester Stallone

- Actor, writer, director known for creating Rocky and Rambo
- Was evicted and homeless for 3 weeks before his film start
- Rocky was nominated for 10 Academy Awards, 2 for Stallone
- Voted into the International Boxing Hall of Fame
- Philadelphia has a permanent Rocky statue near the museum

Rule #1: Get it Done

"What I'll try to do is I write long-handed.

So on legal pad I'll go, 'Goes here. Sees his mother. Goes to the store.'

I'll have like ten things of where he's going. 'Gets on a horse. Goes swimming. Boom, boom, boom.'

And I do that, and I know in my heart, 80% of it will be no good, but you're getting through the screenplay.

You're getting it done because the rewrite is always more fun and much more enjoyable.

I don't believe people should look for perfection, or even 50% perfection in the first draft.

It's always going to be this, like a child scribbling, but you did it.

The main thing for me is to once you have that accomplished, and you can do it in two weeks, three weeks, again, maybe 10% will be good, but you now have this *sense of accomplishment.*

You did it, and the rewriting process starts, and that's when the fun begins."

Rule #2: Just Keep Going

"I truly believe, and people throw the word around, in dreams.

It's all about dreams, and by the way, dreams cost nothing.

They're free.

The hard part is just *keeping them going,* and please keep them going because we're here for one simple reason: *our dreams come true,* and there's no reason every one of yours can't either."

Rule #3: Improvise

"We were running behind schedule and I had to shoot a montage. Oh God. This montage would have taken like five days. So what I did is, I came in there, brought everyone into one big room, all the dancers, and had three cameras.

I took one camera and just stayed with John Travolta, and I worked with him. And the rest, I said to everyone just dance, and do whatever you want, cart wheels. I said catch it all, whatever.

And then I sent a camera down when they're making the stage, and just regular light, and just shoot what you can. No sound or nothing, and we put it all together, and saved four days of filming. *Which none of that, absolutely zero, was choreographed.*

Isn't it funny? I said, 'Okay John, just do this. Cut. Do this. Cut.' I swear to God. And then the other dancers were just over in the corner. One was just scratching, doing a somersault, stretching, and you put it all together.

So there are no rules. It's crazy."

Rule #4: Use Fear to Fuel You

"There's always fear, and I even put it in 'Rocky II,' that, "I'm afraid, I'm afraid." But the *fear is the fuel that we use for overachievement.*

If I wasn't afraid at times, I wouldn't work as hard, because the fear is: I don't want to sit back in mediocrity. I don't want to just say, 'I want to rest on my laurels.'

So I hear footsteps all the time, and I know that I only have a certain amount of time and I don't want to waste it, because *it's gone so quickly.*

There's only a certain amount of productivity in a day and we don't want to waste it."

Rule #5: Love Challenge

Interviewer: "What in this whole world turns you on?"

Sylvester Stallone: *"Challenge. I really just love it.* I love being told, 'No'. It just means, 'Yes.' You know?"

Interviewer: "What turns you off?"

Sylvester Stallone: "Lack of enthusiasm. That really turns me off."

Rule #6: #Believe in Yourself *[Evan's Fav]*

"Originally when I brought the script to them, they were fairly enthusiastic about it. The one thing they were not enthusiastic about *was me playing the part*, and I really can't blame them at the time. Ryan O'Neal was a candidate. Burt Reynolds, Robert Redford, Jimmy Kahn, and they all were at the top of their game. And so I could see it, but there was something inside of me that this opportunity is never going to come around. I really wasn't used to money and I had no idea what I would be missing. But the temptation started to come forward. First it was $25,000, then $100,000, and I go, *'I've never heard of $100,000.'* Because I had like $160 in the bank, and I said I had to sell my dog, and things were not looking very good. My $40 car had just blown up so I was taking a bus to work.

And still it didn't matter. I wanted to stick with it. Then it went up to $150,000, $175,000. Then it went up to $250,000. Now my head was starting to spin. And it went up to $330,000 and I heard it went to $360,000 and I thought, 'Alright, you know, you've really *managed poverty very well*. You've got this down to a science. You really don't need much to live on.' I had sort of figured it out. So I was not in any way used to the good life. So I know in the back of my mind, if I sell this script and it does very, very well, I'm going to jump off a building if I'm not in it. There's no doubt about it. I'm going to leap in front of a train. I'm going to be very, very upset. So this is one of those things where you just roll the dice and say, *'I've got to try it. Just do it. I may be totally wrong but I just believe in it.'"*

Rule #7: Find Your Process

"Writing, I almost oppose it, like exercise.

I get up maybe at 4:30 in the morning, it takes an hour to get going, and then I'll start to **write about three hours.**

And then it becomes repetitive.

The next day I get up, and even if I don't feel inspired, I'll sit for those three hours until the brain says, 'Okay, you must start to produce something. So try to write quickly.'

And I follow a pattern just the way you would if you were in the Army. And then that gets me through it quickly.

Some writers will take a year, two years. Everyone has a different process. But that's what I do.

I use to write at night all the time but I found that everything, everyone died. It was dark, kind of creepy.

It was really horrible, very depressing. Then I realized Edgar Allen Poe used to write at night, and I figured out why."

Rule #8: You Have to Try

"You have to try. **You have to see if you really are what you think you are.**

And by that I mean, I wanted one chance to **prove whether I was a good actor.**

Or that I was a lousy actor. Or whether I should go get a Dairy Queen stand. Or maybe I should get out of acting and I just **needed one vehicle to prove it.**

I had to be up there just enough to say, 'Jesus, you stink Stallone,' or, 'Not bad!'"

Rule #9: You Only Learn Through Failure

"Give up something to get something. I thought I didn't have any money, so I had no phone. I painted my windows black, so I didn't know if the sun was up, the sun was down. All I knew was I had to write. And I wrote, and I wrote, it was very bad. It wasn't good at all. But every day it was getting better and better, like a machine, like a muscle, until *finally the idea of Rocky came.* So the idea is you *must fail 100 times to succeed once.* That's part of it.

No one succeeds the first time. It's learning how to not get disappointed with failure to understand failure. *You only learn when you fail.* You don't learn when you succeed. But when you fail, that's when you learn. How I learned, lucky I was a failure in New York, and that is the reason I started writing, which made me successful. I had to teach myself early on. Expect to fail. Expect it. Covet it. Welcome it. It's going to happen. *But it's not a permanent state.*"

Rule #10: Keep Moving Forward

(From the movie 'Rocky Balboa')

"Somewhere along the line you changed. You stopped being you. You let people stick a finger in your face and tell you you're no good. And when things got hard you started looking for something to blame, like a big shadow. Let me tell you something you already know. *The world ain't all sunshine and rainbows.* It's a very mean and nasty place and I don't care how tough you are it will beat you to your knees and keep you there permanently if you let it.

You, me, or nobody is gonna hit as hard as life. But it ain't how hard you hit. It's about how hard you can get hit, and keep moving forward. How much you can take, and keep moving forward.

That's how winning is done! Now, if you know what you're worth, then go out and get what you're worth. But you gotta be willing to take the hits, and not pointing fingers saying you ain't where you are because of him, or her, or anybody. Cowards do that and that ain't you. You're better than that!"

Sylvester Stallone Summary

1. Get it Done
2. Just Keep Going
3. Improvise
4. Use Fear to Fuel You
5. Love Challenge
6. #Believe in Yourself
7. Find Your Process
8. Do One Thing Right
9. You Only Learn Through Failure
10. Keep Moving Forward

How can you apply these rules to your business or life today?

_____

_____

_____

_____

_____

_____

_____

_____

_____

_____

#DidYouKnow: Sylvester Stallone became a boxing promoter in the 1980s. His boxing promoting company, Tiger Eye Productions, signed world champion boxers Sean O'Grady and Aaron Pryor.

"I know if I keep talking about how dirty it is out here, somebody's going to clean it up." – Tupac Shakur

- Rapper, author, actor, and poet
- Sold over 75 million records globally, one of the all-time bests
- Songs revolved around violence and hardship in inner cities
- Rolling Stone's No. 86 of "100 Immortal Artists of All Time"
- Inducted into the Hip-Hop Hall of Fame in 2002

Rule #1: Be Outspoken

Interviewer: "What do you think you are most known for, your acting, your music, or the controversy that surrounds you?"

Tupac Shakur: "Well, my big mouth. My big mouth. I've got a big mouth. Can't help it. *I talk from my heart, I'm real.*

Whatever comes, comes. But, my controversy probably. It's not my fault. I'm trying to find my way in the world. You know? I'm trying to be somebody instead of just make money off everybody.

I go down paths that haven't been traveled before. And I usually messed up, but I learn. I come back stronger. I'm not talking ignorant.

So I obviously put thought into what I do. So I think my mouth and my controversy. I have not been out of the papers since I joined 'Digital Underground.'

And that's good for me because I don't want to be forgotten. If I'm forgotten, then that means I'm comfortable. And that means that I think that everything is okay."

Rule #2: Search for Knowledge

"My mother taught me three things. *Respect knowledge. Search for knowledge.* It's an eternal journey. That's like my haircut. The line, 360 degrees of knowledge, always. And, she taught me to *not be quiet.* If there's something on my mind, speak it.

She always taught also to listen. And, she told me this little joke, that God give you two ears to listen and one mouth to speak. Two ears and one mouth. Common sense. One mouth. You should speak but you should also listen.

And that's where the knowledge come from. Listening. And once you get the knowledge, then you can speak. And, it helps you. So, she taught me respect, knowledge and understanding. *Mostly just listen a lot.*"

Rule #3: Be a Real Model

"Instead of a role model *I want to be a real model* cause a role is a role. If I be me I can never let anybody down.

I don't want anybody to follow me. I don't want it but what I want you to do is to listen. We've got to stand up at some point and just stop stuttering. *Just say what you mean and say it loud so everybody hears you.* We gotta come out! Say what we got to say!"

Rule #4: Share Abundance

"There's too much money here. I mean nobody should be hitting the lotto for $36 million and we've got people starving in the streets.

That is not idealistic, it's just real. That is just stupid.

There's no way Michael Jackson should have or *whoever should have a million thousand druple billion dollars and then* have people starving.

There's no way. There's no way that these people should own planes and there are people who don't have houses.

Apartments, shacks, drawers, pants. I know you rich.

I know you got $40 billion, but can you just keep it to one house? You only need one house. And if you only got two kids, can you just keep it to two rooms?

I mean why have 52 rooms and you know there's somebody with no rooms? It just don't make sense to me. It don't.

And then these people celebrate Christmas. They got big trees, huge trees, all the little trimmings, everybody got gifts, and there's somebody that's starving.

And they're having a white Christmas. They're having a great Christmas. Egg Nog and the whole nine. *That's not fair to me.*"

Rule #5: Spark a Change in the World [Evan's Fav]

"All this society is doing is leeching off the ghetto. They use the ghetto for their pain, for their sorrow, for their culture, for their music, for their happiness, for their movies, to talk about 'Boyz in the Hood.'

I don't want to be 50 years old at a BET we shall overcome achievement awards. *Uh uh, not me.*

I want when they see me, they know that every day that I'm breathing, it's for us to go farther. Every time when I speak, I want the truth to come out. Every time I speak I want a shiver.

I don't want them to know what I'm going to say because it's polite. They know what I'm going to say.

Even if I get in trouble, ain't that what we're supposed to do?

I'm not saying I'm going to rule the world, or I'm going to change the world, but I guarantee that *I will spark the brain that will change the world.*

That's our job, to spark somebody else watching us. We might not be the ones, but let's not be selfish. And because we not going to change the world, let's not talk about how we should change it.

I don't know how to change it. *But I know if I keep talking about how dirty it is out here, somebody's going to clean it up.*"

Rule #6: Get Up and Keep Trying

"God ain't finished with me yet. There's a path for me. I make mistakes and I might fall, but I'm *gonna get up and I keep trying because I believe* in it.

And that's ghetto, you know, to do what you feel. It's not all pretty, but it's still what I feel. It's still from my soul, my heart."

Rule #7: Shine

"I can't explain why I shine and no one else shines. *I think everybody shines, in different things.* And there's a lot of things I can't do. I can't play basketball like every black person in America. But I can act. I know how to go to that true spot, because I'm there every day I can be me. I can be whoever because I'm true to me. I can go to neutral easy. A lot of people, black, white, Mexican, young or old, fat or skinny have a problem being true to themselves. *They have a problem looking in the mirror and looking directly into their own souls.*

The reason I sell six million records. The reason I can go to jail and come out without a scratch. The reason I can walk around. The reason I am who I am today is because I can look directly into my face and find my soul. It's there. It's not sold. I didn't sell it. It's still within me. I still feel it. *My heart is still connected to my body.* So any character I can bring that intensity, that truth, that honesty to it. So, it's not really tricky. Everybody can do it if they just go to that spot. I guess all the things that happen to me in my life allow me to go there easy."

Rule #8: Talk About Problems

"If I know that in this hotel room they have food every day and I'm knocking on the door every day to eat. Open the door. Let me see the party. Let me see them throwing salami all over, just throwing food around. They're telling me there's no food in here.

Every day, I'm standing outside trying to sing my way in. *'We are hungry please let us in.* We are hungry please let us in.' After about a week that song is going to change to 'We are hungry, we need some food.' After two or three weeks, it's like, 'Give me all your food,' knocking down doors. After a year, I'm just picking the lock, coming through the door, blasting. Now, what do you think we're going to do?

I'm rapping to my community. *In the media they don't talk about it, so in my raps I have to talk about it."*

258

Rule #9: Learn From Tough Times

"My mother had a really bad childhood. And my father had a bad childhood. And I had a bad childhood. **But I love my childhood. Even though it was bad,** I love it.

I feel like it's taught me so much. And I feel like nothing can phase me. Nothing in this world, **nothing, can surprise me.** It might set me back, but only momentarily. Only to spring back.

I think it's helped me to learn. It really did help me to learn. And since my mother had a bad childhood, she knows the importance of being honest. And the importance **of facing each situation as it comes.** And not dealing in a fairytale land.

Being realistic about the problem, and analyzing it, and solving it. Seeing what you can do to solve it. So, if you have a happy childhood, you tend to want your child to have a happy childhood.

You tend to want to keep the bad things out, and I don't think that's good because then you're not prepared for the world."

Rule #10: Do Something

"All B.S. aside, it all comes down to we got to survive. I mean, even warriors put their spears down on Sundays. We've got to survive here in this country because I'm not going back to Africa. We've got to survive here.

For us to survive here, white folks, black folks, Korean folks, Mexican folks, Puerto Ricans, we've got to understand each other. **We've got to take a bigger chance.**

And when I say Americans, people think I'm talking about Uncle Sam.

I mean, you, you, you.

I mean you need to do something."

Tupac Shakur Summary

1. Be Outspoken
2. Search for Knowledge
3. Be a Real Model
4. Share Abundance
5. Spark a Change in the World
6. Get Up and Keep Trying
7. Shine
8. Talk About Problems
9. Learn From Tough Times
10. Do Something

How can you apply these rules to your business or life today?

_____

_____

_____

_____

_____

_____

_____

_____

_____

_____

_____

#DidYouKnow: Forbes recognized Tupac Shakur as a "Top-Earning Dead Celebrity," coming in at number 10 on their list.

"You will have many opportunities to reinvent yourself. It's worthwhile taking risks." – Sundar Pichai

- Business executive, CEO of Google
- Holds an M.S. from Stanford and an MBA from Wharton
- Joined Google in 2004 to lead Chrome product management
- In 2014 was considered for Microsoft CEO position
- In 2015 was selected to be Google CEO

Rule #1: Think About What's Next

"The world keeps changing so a big part of what I focus on at any given time is making sure we are innovating and building products for the future.

It's just got to be a normal course of how you think.

And so we are constantly thinking about *what to do next.*

Android is very popular. People are using smartphones.

But I always sit and think about what is the next version of how people will use computing?

So we are thinking about things like virtual reality or *augmented reality.*

These are all new areas, but we are constantly thinking about it.

You have to do that on a *constant basis to push forward."*

Rule #2: Enable People

"The thing which attracted me to Google and to Internet in general is that it's a *great equalizer.*

So to me, I've always been struck by the fact that Google search worked the same, as long as you had access to a computer with connectivity.

If you were a rural kid anywhere or if you were a professor at Stanford or Harvard.

To me, I want Google to strive to push to do that, not just build technology for certain segments.

For me it matters that we drive *technology as an equalizing force, as an enabler to everyone around the world."*

Rule #3: Ideas Matter

"Growing up in India, like many of you, I got my first telephone when I was 12. In my case, it turned out to be a rotary phone, so it wasn't that great for selfies. But I still loved to call my friends, play with it, and sometimes take it apart. That telephone cemented my fascination with technology.

I remember in my parents' house in Chennai, reading about the invention of the **transistor at Bell Labs.** Of course, that initial invention helped found what became known as Silicon Valley, and out of that came companies like Fairchild Semiconductor and Intel, and all the computers and software that we all use today.

You can **draw a direct line from that invention** to the technology that powers your Twitter feed or your WeChat messages today. I remember reading about that and thinking, 'It's the idea that matters.'

It didn't matter where you come from, or what your background is. **One revolutionary idea, one brilliant invention, can unleash other entrepreneurs to revolutionize industries in ways you could never predict."**

Rule #4: Take Risks *[Evan's Fav]*

"You will have many, many opportunities to reinvent yourself. So I think it's worthwhile taking risks and trying to do something you're really excited by.

If at the first attempt you don't do it, you can try again and things tend to work out in the long run. In Silicon Valley, part of the reason so many people start up a company is, starting up a company and even having failed, you can wear it like a badge of honor. I think that's important, culturally, **risk is rewarded.** I remember when I started working at Google, if I went and people were discussing ideas, the other people who heard the ideas try to build on those ideas. They encourage you. So it's a **culture of optimism.** It's a culture of risk taking and I think that's really important."

Rule #5: Be an Optimist

"I've always been very passionate, so *I'm an optimist* about how technology can make a difference.

I focus on that, and that way you tend to forget about the other things. The rest is noise."

Rule #6: Solve Problems

"We believe that software is at a stage where software increasingly is playing a more and more *critical role in solving things,* which it didn't before.

So to me when I look at cars, people spend an inordinate amount of time in cars.

These are resources which are very poorly utilized.

Right now as we speak, you can look outside and you can see all the cars which are parked.

They get used less than 10%.

We see these problems, and we say, *'Okay, can we solve it at scale,* and does computing play a part in it, software, and computer science?'

And while the effort may seem ambitious or crazy, we take a very disciplined approach inside. Those are thought through like businesses which we are building.

It's just that we are willing to *take a long term view,* but we run them in a very disciplined way.

Our research can be longer term, and we never know whether some of them even make viable business applications, but we want to push the technology because you don't know what's possible on the other side."

Rule #7: Design for Everyone

"When Larry and Sergey founded Google Search, one of the things that struck me is that it was *available for everyone to use.*

We deeply desire our services to work for everyone.

And that inherently means we have to work with partners.

That is the thesis underlying *everything we do.*"

Rule #8: Have a Good Morning Routine

Interviewer: "What is your morning routine like? What do you do when you first get up in the morning?"

Sundar Pichai: "Believe it or not I still, *I read a physical paper every single morning.* I read the Wall Street Journal every morning. I read the New York Times online.

And I still am very *particular about having my tea.* It's very English.

I'm vegetarian, so I need to get my protein.

I always have an omelet in the morning with toast, tea, and read my paper, so I do that *every morning."*

Interviewer: "What time do you wake up?"

Sundar Pichai: *"6:30 to 7:00,* so that's when I do it."

Interviewer: "Do you exercise in the morning?"

Sundar Pichai: "No, later in the day sometimes if I get a chance, but always in the evening. I wish I could do it in the morning.

I'm not a morning person so I need my time with my paper and tea to wake up and get going."

265

Rule #9: Always Aim High

"I think we've always had an **ambitious approach** to it.

We call it internally '10x' or 'Moonshots.'

We try to work on things which people will use every day, will apply to billions of people, and it solves a real problem for people.

So that's the bar. So, anything we try to do, we think of it that way, and so we **aim high.** We try to use deep computer science to anything we approach so that we can have a differentiated approach to solving it.

You want to **aim high enough that you fail a few times.** I think that's a natural part of the process. In fact, Larry used to say 'If you work on really difficult things you're better off because you have no competition.

Others aren't working on that difficult a problem. And even if you fail, you **end up doing something great in process.** "

Rule #10: Push Yourself

"I would actually encourage all of you, if at some point in your life you have to work with **people where you feel a bit insecure.**

That's essential, because that means you're working with people who are better than you, and who are pushing you.

I will always encourage you, if you actually feel very secure in what you do, that means you're doing something comfortable and **not pushing yourself.**

There are many many times I've felt, working with people and a group, 'Am I doing enough? These people seem much better than me.'

I think that's an **inherent part of learning.**"

Sundar Pichai Summary

1. Think About What's Next
2. Enable People
3. Ideas Matter
4. Take Risks
5. Be an Optimist
6. Solve Problems
7. Design for Everyone
8. Have a Good Morning Routine
9. Always Aim High
10. Push yourself

How can you apply these rules to your business or life today?

_____

_____

_____

_____

_____

_____

_____

_____

_____

_____

#DidYouKnow: Sundar Pichai is a Futbol Club Barcelona fan and watches all their games.

"If you praise people they flourish, and that's the critical attribute of a leader." – **Sir Richard Branson**

- Founded Virgin Group, which controls over 400 companies
- Knighted in England for his services to entrepreneurship
- Named as the No. 1 LGBT ally by OUTstanding
- An experienced kitesurfer, holding world records in the sport
- Pledged to invest $3 billion to address global warming

Rule #1: Keep it Simple

"I am dyslexic and therefore I think I've been very good at **keeping things simple because, as a dyslexic,** I need things to be simple for myself, and therefore Virgin.

I think, when we launch a financial service company or a bank we do not use jargon.

Everything is very clear cut, very simple, and I think people have an affinity to the Virgin brand because we don't talk above them or talk down to them."

Rule #2: Give it a Try [Evan's Fav]

"I think that lots of people **do not have the courage to try to start a business.**

I've written the book called **'Screw It Just Do It,'** and it basically is trying to say to people, just give it a try.

Sometimes a very, very small amount of money is all that's needed to start a company.

My mother found a bracelet on the street and she handed it in to the police station.

After three months the police let her sell it.

The couple of hundred dollars was really critical at a critical time in the development of our business.

So all I say is just give it a go and good luck."

Rule #3: Be a Leader

"That I think the most important thing about running a company is to remember all the time what a company is.

A company is simply a group of people, and as a leader of people, you have to be a *great listener.* You have to be a great motivator. You have to be very good at *praising and looking for the best in people.*

People are no different from flowers.

If you water flowers they flourish.

If you praise people they flourish, and that's the critical attribute of a leader."

Rule #4: Don't Give Up

"There is a *very thin dividing line between success and failure* when you start a business from scratch and if you don't have enough money to pay the bills, you go the wrong side of that dividing line.

If you can somehow get enough money to pay the bills you stay the right side of that dividing line.

I've always been running. Either running faster than perhaps I should and I have great difficulty saying no to things so I keep on taking on new things. We've just managed to stay the right side of the dividing line over the last 50 years of business.

But equally in those early days when you're starting a business without any financial backing, it's easy to slip the wrong side, and, in fact, most entrepreneurs do slip the wrong side and the important thing is then just *pick yourself up and start again.*

And if it *doesn't work at that time then keep going until you do succeed, and not to give up."*

Rule #5: Delegate

"The next stage is to be a **great delegator** and not try and do everything yourself.

Try to find people who are better than you.

All the time try to find people who are better than you to put you out of business effectively.

So whatever you are spending all your day doing, try to find someone who's better than you to do that, to replace you at it, so that you can go off and think about the next big picture.

An entrepreneur is not a manager.

An entrepreneur is somebody who **is great at conceiving ideas, starting ideas, building ideas,** but then handing over to really good managers to manage the businesses.

The moment you've got more than one business you can't be hands on doing everything."

Rule #6: Treat People Well

"I don't actually think that the stereotype of a businessperson trading away with people to get to the top, generally speaking, works.

I think if you treat people well, people will come back for more.

And it's a very small world.

I actually think that the best way of becoming a successful business leader is **dealing with people fairly and well.**

And I'd like to think that's how we run Virgin."

Rule #7: Shake Things Up

"I love learning.

I've never actually thought I was starting a company as such.

I just saw situations as I traveled in life where I felt I could improve on the way things that have been done by other people.

So, one of my favorite phrases is, 'Screw it let's do it,' and I've used that phrase a lot of times.

And we just *love going in and trying to shake up industries* and doing it better than it's been done before."

Rule #8: People Will Be Skeptical

"When we launched Virgin Atlantic 30 years ago the 'New York Times' did a review.

They did some market research and they said, first of all, with a name like Virgin it's not going to go the whole way.

But secondly, they did market research where it said only seven percent of people would fly on a airline called Virgin, and we put our hands up and said, *seven percent would be just fine.*

So we carried on with it, but there were a lot of skeptics out there and there *always will be lots of skeptics when you want to start something new.*

Everybody will tell you why it's a bad idea, why you shouldn't do it, why you'll lose everything you've got, and in the end you've just *got to try to prove them wrong."*

Rule #9: Affect Lives Positively

"I think the word 'business,' it becomes a business, but what you're doing is you're painting a picture. *You're trying to create something to make a difference in other people's lives.*

You have a blank canvas and you're filling in every little bit of that canvas to get every single little detail right. And if that canvas *sings out at you* at the end and it's a beautiful picture, your business is going to be successful.

If bits of the canvas are not quite right, your business may fail. So if you set out to change people's lives, you've got to get every single little detail right. You've got to make sure that the *people that you're working with 100% believe in what you're trying* to do and you've got to make sure that what you're trying to do is worthwhile spending your time on.

And at the end of the day you want to be sure that the people's lives you've affected. You've really bettered it. You've affected them and benefited them. And if you get all that right, hopefully you'll be able to pay the bills at the end of the year."

Rule #10: Play Hard, Work Hard

"*Life is short and it should be fun.* If the Chairman of the company is having fun, if you go to a party, if I let my hair down, and I'm the first to be thrown in the swimming pool and I'm not just standing in the corner of the room sipping sherry or something, then everybody will have a laugh and everybody will have fun.

If you're Chairman of the company, be the first to dance on the table, just get everybody else up dancing on the table.

Make sure the *party is a laugh.* So play hard, and work hard, and follow certain principles in life.

Love people. Make sure you make a positive difference in this world while you're on it."

Sir Richard Branson Summary

1. Keep it Simple
2. Give it a Try
3. Be a Leader
4. Don't Give Up
5. Delegate
6. Treat People Well
7. Shake Things Up
8. People Will Be Skeptical
9. Affect Lives Positively
10. Play Hard, Work Hard

How can you apply these rules to your business or life today?

_____

_____

_____

_____

_____

_____

_____

_____

_____

_____

_____

#DidYouKnow: In the 1980s, Sir Richard Branson was briefly given the post of 'litter Tsar' by UK Prime Minister Margaret Thatcher, charged with keeping Britain tidy.

"Be brutally honest with yourself. You've got to know your business better than anybody." – Mark Cuban

- Entrepreneur, investor, TV personality and philanthropist
- Known for being an investor on the TV Show 'Shark Tank'
- Owner of the NBA's Dallas Mavericks, Magnolia Pictures
- At age 12 he sold garbage bags to pay for a pair of shoes
- In 1999 his dot com business was bought for $5.7 billion

Rule #1: Now Is the Time

"Personally I think every time is a perfect time to start a business. There's no bad time.

If you do the work, if you do the **preparation**, you'll know when it's time. And it doesn't mean that it won't be a little bit scary, but you'll know.

You don't have to quit the daytime job if you don't feel all that comfortable and you can give it a run at night.

But, whatever works for you, now with the Internet, you've got all the choices in the world and you can *just go out there and do your own thing."*

Rule #2: Be Passionate

"The passion I've always had for business and being an entrepreneur, that transfers into the Mavs.

I've always been passionate.

Some people thought it's more OCD than anything else, which I think is a great trait for an entrepreneur.

I mentioned the **stamp business**.

I would stay up until three, four in the morning, even though I had to get up and go to school, and read 'Linn's Stamp News' and 'Scott's Stamp Journals' and have them all memorized and use that to get myself an edge.

Even when I was in college, I'd be in the library reading business books and just looking for business biographies and just reading all I could about business.

When I had Micro Solutions and I started with no money, I'd pull all-nighters in front of borrowed computers teaching myself software and how to program."

Rule #3: Don't Make Excuses *[Evan's Fav]*

"Just to go after it. I mean, the thing about being an entrepreneur is it's just all you.

A lot of *people like to make excuses,* 'I don't have connections, I don't have money, I don't have this,' but if you find something that you like to do or love to do, be great at it and see if you can turn it into a business and, worst case, you're going to have fun doing what it is you love to do, and best case you can turn it into a business.

I'm just not big on excuses, I just think that everybody has that opportunity to go for it. They've just got to do it."

Rule #4: Learn from History

"One of the things that companies do or startups do, they come up with an idea, they'll Google it, and if they don't see it in the first two pages, they think it's original.

You've *got to go back,* because over the past 15 years there's so many different businesses that have tried and failed.

You have to go back and find those and learn from those. You've got to understand all the implications and you have to learn from history.

And so, the best advice I can give you, before talking to you or emailing with you, is that *you've got to find out the history of people who have tried your idea.*

There's a 99.99999% chance that your idea's been tried before.

That's not a good reason not to start it, because you might be able to outperform them, but you better learn from the history of your idea.

Because you know what they say about people who don't learn from history."

Rule #5: Enjoy Competing

"I've always just really enjoyed just the **competition of business.** I think in the sports business I'll talk to our players and it'll be like, 'Well you guys compete for 48 minutes and you practice a couple hours and you work on your game independently a couple hours, but **the ultimate sport is business,** because you have to compete with everybody. And you have to do it 24 by seven by 365 days a year forever and there's always somebody out there trying to kick your butt.'

There's always somebody who looks at your business and says, 'I can do that better. I have a better idea.' And you have to compete with that person and all the while you have to make your customers happy, your employees happy.

It's the competitive side of me, in any entrepreneur, that I think that has to drive you and I think that carries over into the Mavericks. **I want to win and I want to compete.**"

Rule #6: Know Your Business

"99% of small businesses you can start with next to no capital. It's more about effort. **Small businesses don't fail for lack of capital. They fail for lack of brains. They fail for lack of effort.** Most people just aren't willing to put in the time to work smart.

They go for it in a lot of cases but they just don't recognize how much work's involved.

And if you do the preparation, if you start a business, you better know your industry and your company better than anyone in the whole wide world, because you're competing. And to think that whoever it is you're competing with is just going to let you come in and take their business...

Obviously that's naive and I think most people don't recognize that. If you're going to compete with me and one of my businesses, you better realize that I'm working 24 hours a day to kick your ass."

Rule #7: Be Brutally Honest with Yourself

"One of the big things that all startups do is they lie to themselves over and over and over. 'Mine's faster, mine's cheaper, mine's better, mine's this, mine's that.' No it's not. And the reason it's not is because whoever it is you're competing with, it's not like they're ignoring you. It's not like, 'Oh my goodness, this guy just started on Shopify in this startup competition. He's doing a million dollars this year. Woe is me. I might as well close up the doors.'

What are they doing? 'I'm going to copy what they're doing,' and now you've got to stay ahead. And so, you've got to be very careful as an entrepreneur to be **brutally honest with yourself** and those are some of the things that you'll hear from me as a mentor. That know what you know. Know what you don't know. **But you've got to know your business better than anybody.**"

Rule #8: Know Your Strengths and Weaknesses

"I think most important is **knowing your strengths and weaknesses and knowing what you enjoy doing.** If you look at it as a job, you've already lost. It's not going to be your passion, and you're going to count the hours. If you look at it as something you love to do, and then you know what your strengths are, then you can leverage those strengths in your business and in helping others. **And once you recognize your weaknesses, then you can work with people that compliment you.**

Every one of my businesses I've had a partner who is very anal. I mean, incredibly anal people, **perfectionists**, because I'm a slob. I'm a big picture, think about what's around the corner, how is technology going to change things, how can I change this industry and making sure that there's somebody there to dot the i's, cross the t's, and keep me in the base lines.

And **recognizing my weaknesses is just as important as recognizing my strengths and my core competencies and having a passion to do them.**"

Rule #9: Be Unique

"You've got to be **differentiated and unique.** You've got to know what your **core competency** is and be great at it. I think what people fail to realize is that there's got to be a defining feature of your company and you've got to be the best in the world at that. Whatever industry you're in, if you don't know more about it than anybody else in the world, whoever those other people are that know more are going to kick your ass."

Rule #10: Be Yourself

"I got a job working for a company called Your Business Software. We sold software and I didn't know anything about software. I took one computer class in Indiana and kind of cheated to pass.

I figured computers were new and technology was new. This technology was new so nobody had a head start on me because it was changing so rapidly like it is today, that if I just put in the time I can learn as much as anybody else. And so I taught myself. I'd stay up late reading software manuals, taught myself different little simple programming languages and kept on getting bigger and bigger and better and better, but it was at a retail store.

One of my responsibilities was to come in and sweep the floor, wipe down the windows and open the store. And I had a customer who wanted me to come out there and close a deal. And it was a $15,000 deal, $1,500 dollar commission to me. Told my boss, he said, 'No, you need to be there to open the store.' And I made the executive decision that I was going to go get the check, because I was living with **six guys in a three bedroom apartment, sleeping on the floor,** and this check meant I could not use the same Holiday Inn towels with holes in them that I'd stolen.

So I went and picked up the check, thinking when I came back and gave the check to my boss all would be forgiven and sales cures all. Fired me. Fired me! And so those experiences confirmed what I already knew, that I was a sh** ass employee and that I better start my own."

Mark Cuban Summary

1. Now is the Time
2. Be Passionate
3. Don't Make Excuses
4. Learn from History
5. Enjoy Competing
6. Know Your Business
7. Be Brutally Honest with Yourself
8. Know Your Strengths and Weaknesses
9. Be Unique
10. Be Yourself

How can you apply these rules to your business or life today?

_____

_____

_____

_____

_____

_____

_____

_____

_____

_____

_____

#DidYouKnow: In 2003, Mark Cuban founded the Fallen Patriot Fund to help families of US military killed or injured during the Iraq War.

YOUR TOP 10 RULES FOR SUCCESS

You've just finished reading 400 rules for success (500 if you sent in your receipt or picture). Now it's time to write the rules for success for the most important person, **YOU.**

Use the space below to write down which 10 rules you want to live by. Use them as *daily inspiration* for the person that you are and are continually becoming.

1) _____

2) _____

3) _____

4) _____

5) _____

6) _____

7) _____

8) _____

9) _____

10) _____

THE END

Congratulations on reaching the end! Here are a few ideas for you to consider:

1) If you haven't emailed your receipt or a picture of you with the book yet, send it to <u>top10@evancarmichael.com</u> to get your *free bonuses.*

2) The lessons here are habits of success. You don't absorb everything by reading it once. Start the book over again. *Make it a habit of reading one page per day.* If you read a page a day and take action on what you read it'll change your life.

3) I'd love to have your help spreading the message. If you liked the book *please consider sharing it* with your friends and online so that more people can learn the wisdom here that is essential but not taught in schools.

4) If you got great value from this book consider buying a copy for a friend. Some people are making this book a part of their customer service where all new customers get a copy of the book as a thank you. If it made a meaningful difference for you, it'll make a meaningful difference for others and *you'll be remembered* as the person who introduced them to it.

5) Most importantly of all, *take action.* Don't let this book just sit on your shelf collecting dust. Do something. You don't get changes in your life or business by just reading. You get changes by taking action.

I can't wait to see and hear about your progress. You're going to change the world and I'm honored to play a tiny part in your journey.

Much love,

Evan.
#Believe

ABOUT EVAN CARMICHAEL

Evan Carmichael #Believes in entrepreneurs. At nineteen, he built then sold a biotech software company. At twenty-two, he was a venture capitalist helping raise $500 thousand to $15 million. Evan was named one of the Top 100 Great Leadership Speakers for your Next Conference by Inc. Magazine and one of the Top 40 Social Marketing Talents by Forbes. He has been interviewed or featured as an entrepreneur expert in the New York Times, the Wall Street Journal, Forbes, Mashable, and elsewhere. He runs EvanCarmichael.com, a popular YouTube channel for entrepreneurs, and his first book was Your One Word: The Powerful Secret to Creating a Business and Life That Matter. He speaks globally and is based in Toronto.

And his One Word is #Believe. What's yours?